Strong Reasons

Ken Chant

Strong Reasons

Ken Chant

Copyright © 2015 Ken Chant

Revised Edition 2015

ISBN 978-1-61529-153-3

Vision Publishing
1672 Main Street E 109
Ramona, CA 92065
1 800-9-VISION
www.booksbyvision.com

All Rights Reserved Worldwide.

No part of this book may be reproduced in any manner except by the written permission of the author, except in brief quotations embodied in critical articles of review.

A Note on Gender

It is unfortunate that the English language does not contain an adequate generic pronoun (especially in the singular number) that includes without bias both male and female. So "he, him, his, man, mankind," with their plurals, must do the work for both sexes. Accordingly, wherever it is appropriate to do so in the following pages, please include the feminine gender in the masculine, and vice versa.

Footnotes

A work once fully referenced will thereafter be noted either by "ibid" or "op. cit."

Abbreviations

Abbreviations commonly used for the books of the Bible are

Genesis	Ge	Habakkuk	Hb
Exodus	Ex	Zephaniah	Zp
Leviticus	Le	Haggai	Hg
Numbers	Nu	Zechariah	Zc
Deuteronomy	De	Malachi	Mal
Joshua	Js		
Judges	Jg		
Ruth	Ru	Matthew	Mt
1 Samuel	1 Sa	Mark	Mk
2 Samuel	2 Sa	Luke	Lu
1 Kings	1 Kg	John	Jn
2 Kings	2 Kg	Acts	Ac
1 Chronicles	1 Ch	Romans	Ro
2 Chronicles	2 Ch	1 Corinthians	1 Co
Ezra	Ezr	2 Corinthians	2 Co
Nehemiah	Ne	Galatians	Ga
Esther	Es	Ephesians	Ep
Job	Jb	Philippians	Ph
Psalm	Ps	Colossians	Cl
Proverbs	Pr	1 Thessalonians	1 Th
Ecclesiastes	Ec	2 Thessalonians	2 Th
Song of Songs	Ca *	1 Timothy	1 Ti
Isaiah	Is	2 Timothy	2 Ti
Jeremiah	Je	Titus	Tit
Lamentations	La	Philemon	Phm
Ezekiel	Ez	Hebrews	He
Daniel	Da	James	Ja
Hosea	Ho	1 Peter	1 Pe
Joel	Jl	2 Peter	2 Pe
Amos	Am	1 John	1 Jn
Obadiah	Ob	2 John	2 Jn
Jonah	Jo	3 John	3 Jn
Micah	Mi	Jude	Ju
Nahum	Na	Revelation	Re

- ♦ Ca is an abbreviation of Canticles, a derivative of the Latin name of the Song of Solomon, which is sometimes also called the Song of Songs.

Scripture translations unless otherwise noted are my own.

Table of Contents

Part One   *The Bible & Science* 5
    Something To Remember 6
    Hardly A Philosopher 7
    Chapter One   Unassailable Fact? 9
    Addendum   Never Say Never 29
    Chapter Two   Unprovable Assumptions 31
    Addendum   Primitive England 55
    Chapter Three   More Assumptions 59
    Chapter Four   A Sense Of Wonder 79
    Addenda   Is There An Objective Reality? 101
Part Two   *The Proofs Of God* 111
    Chapter Five   The Soul's Left Hand 112
    Chapter Six   The Argument From Design 129
    Addendum   Pascal's Wager 145
    Chapter Seven   The Argument From Existence 147
    Chapter Eight   Men, Women, And Morals 159
    Chapter Nine   Community And Cosmos 177
    Addenda   All Things Wise And Wonderful 199
    Conclusion   Faith Is A Choice 203

PART ONE

THE BIBLE & SCIENCE

SOMETHING TO REMEMBER

Although in the first two parts of this book I refer often to "science" in a generic sense, and may sometimes seem to suggest that science has been (or is) opposed to the Christian faith, I certainly do not intend to include all scientists in such expressions. There is no way to invoke the authority of "scientists" as a single class of experts. Men and women engaged in scientific work are spread across a wide spectrum of society, and belong to many different cultural and spiritual groups. There are thousands of scientists (including some from the highest echelons) who are devout Christians. They see no incompatibility between their faith and their science. Nor do I. The greatest discoveries of modern science do not disparage faith; rather, they are harmonious with it.

Someone has said that the first man, Adam, was also the first scientist, because his first task was a scientific one: he had to name the animals! That meant much more than merely giving them a title. Rather, it required Adam to analyse, identify, and understand each creature, then to give it a name appropriate to its nature and function. Whether you hold to a literal or figurative meaning of the story of Adam and Eve, it shows that the scientific enterprise lies under a mandate from heaven.

HARDLY A PHILOSOPHER

"There is nothing so ridiculous but some philosopher has said it."[1]

"One cannot conceive anything so strange and so implausible that it has not already been said by one philosopher or another."[2]

I have a secret dread. While this book shreds what I think are the follies of others, it may happen that I am myself not without sin. Someone more learned than I in philosophy or physics may find my own ignorance brazenly standing in these pages. If so, he or she may be tempted to throw the slur back to me: "There is nothing so absurd but some preacher will spout it!" I hope not. Yet I must admit that I am neither physicist, scientist, nor philosopher. In those fields no higher status belongs to me than that of a reasonably well-read and intelligent layman. While I have done my homework as well as I can, I hardly expect to be free of all error. So if you find a piece of nonsense mixed in with what I trust will be mostly wisdom, please be charitable. Any straightening you may like to do of crooked places will be welcome.

Someone may ask: "If you are not competent, why then did you write the book?" Ah, but I did not say that I lacked competence, only that I am a layman. A problem often comes with books written by experts: only experts can understand them. But I am an ordinary man writing for ordinary people. My only advantage has been God's gift of time and opportunity.

---

[1] De Divinatione II.119; Cicero (B.C. 106-43)
[2] Discourse on Method II; Descartes (1637)

The above remarks, however, should be confined to those pages that employ physics and philosophy to present rational arguments for Christian belief. Other parts of the book deal with biblical ideas, and are more familiar territory. There, after forty years of ministry, I may reasonably claim to speak with higher authority.

Above all, I stand with you as a searcher after truth, yet one who recognises that all truth, whether sacred or secular, ultimately derives from God and must therefore be harmonious with his nature and will. May he then, who is the Truth, open our minds to perceive his imperishable wisdom.

Chapter One

UNASSAILABLE FACT?

More than three hundred years ago an anonymous poet shrewdly observed that scholars are prone to see what they want to see -

> Three wise men of Gotham,
> As I have heard some say,
> Would needs go forth a-hunting
> Upon St David's day.
>
> And all the day they hunted,
> And nothing could they find,
> But an owl in a hollow tree,
> And that they left behind.
>
> One said it was an owl,
> The other he said, Nay;
> The third said 'twas an old man,
> And his beard growing grey.[3]

Such wise men they were! Only one of them saw what was really there (an owl), and even he rode away from it, for it was not what he wanted to see! That syndrome can still be observed. We are all guilty to some extent, but the learned are sometimes particularly prone to a blinkered view -

> "Too much light often blinds gentlemen of this sort.
> They cannot see the forest for the trees."[4]

---

[3] The poem runs to many more stanzas, and has many versions, with the oldest known printing dating from the late 16th. century.

[4] C. M. Wieland (1733-1814); Musarion, Canto II.

But now even the most closed-minded are finding it increasingly difficult to stay myopic. An avalanche of discoveries is demolishing many of the old verities and calling into question almost every aspect of scientific dogmatism. But don't take my word for it. Here is one example of what some noted scientists are saying about mistaken concepts of their work -

> "Scientists are regarded as supermen. They can do anything, given enough money ... In such moonbeams there is a misconception about scientists and the nature of science. But carried within this there is still another misconception, much more serious. This is the misconception that scientists can establish a complete set of facts and relations about the universe, all neatly proved, and that on this formal basis men can securely establish their personal philosophy, their personal religion, free from doubt or error ...

> *"Science never proves anything, in an absolute sense* ... Science *has* come a long way, in delineating the probable nature of the universe that surrounds us, of the physical world in which we live, of our own structure, our physical and chemical nature. ... Then it comes to the questions of consciousness and free will - and there it stops. *No longer can science prove, or even bear evidence.* Those who base their personal philosophies or their religion upon science are left, beyond that point, without support. They end where

they began [5]... *Science proves nothing absolutely. On the most vital questions it does not even produce evidence ...*

"Young men, who will formulate the deep thought of the next generation, should lean on science, for it can teach much and it can inspire. But they should not lean where it does not apply ...

"And the theologian: he can accept the aid of science, which draws for him a wide universe in all its majesty, with life in all its awe-inspiring complexity. He can accept this, knowing that on the central mysteries science cannot speak. And he can step beyond to lead men in paths of righteousness and in paths of peace...

"And the young man ... he will follow science where it leads, but will not attempt to follow where it cannot lead. And, with a pause, he will admit a faith." [6]

Faith? What has science to do with faith? As it happens, a great deal. Yet in popular imagination science and faith are

---

[5] A discovery expressed long ago by Omar Khayyam (c. 1100) in his Rubaiyat:

"Myself when young did eagerly frequent
Doctor and Saint, and heard great argument
About it and about: but evermore
Came out by the same door as in I went.

Why, all the Saints and Sages who discuss'd
Of the Two Worlds so learnedly, are thrust
Like foolish Prophets forth; their words to Scorn
Are scatter'd, and their Mouths are stopt with Dust"
- tr. by Edward Fitzgerald

[6] Dr Vannevar Bush, honorary board chairman of MIT, in an article "Science Pauses" in the May 1965 issue of Fortune magazine. Emphasis mine.

about as compatible as sugar and sand. Mix them together and you spoil both! But without faith - and a large dollop of it - there would be no science. The entire enterprise (as we shall see) rests upon several leaps of faith. Indeed, where science is rightly understood, it should lead irresistibly on toward that highest faith of all - trust in the living God. Does not the scripture say -

> *"The heavens declare the glory of God, and the skies reveal his handiwork. Day after day brings its message; night after night bears faithful witness. ... Their testimony goes out across the whole earth; their words reach to the end of time." (Ps 19:1)*

> *"What can be known about God has been made plain to all mankind, for God himself has shown it to them. From the time the world was first created his limitless power and eternal nature, which were invisible, have been made visible, and able to be understood, by the things he has made. So they are without excuse." (Ro 1:19-20)*

Many scientists heartily agree with such scriptures. Their work is not darkened, but rather illuminated by their faith.

But then what will you do with those other arresting comments? "Science never proves anything in an absolute sense ... On the most vital questions, it does not even produce evidence." *In our society, where for millions of people science has become the true religion, reducing all other faiths to fairy tales, such sentiments from a leading scientist must seem incredible. Yet they are not unusual. Similar pronounce-ments (you will find examples below) are appearing ever more frequently in scientific journals and speeches.*

So then is science fact or myth? Does it support the Bible or destroy it? Does it have any connection with religious truth? Has it made the church obsolete, turning Christians into quaint relics of an outdated superstition? Do we show willful ignorance when we cling to God? Has science really turned the very idea of God into an antique irrelevance?

But perhaps the reverse is true? Perhaps it is now science that finds itself battered? Many are accusing it of dogmatism and of refusing to face reality. Voices are speaking against the falsity of many of its former claims. Perhaps then it is science that has lost its way. Is there now an opportunity for religion to rush back in and reclaim the loyalty of the masses? What should a Christian's attitude be toward these things?

I hope the following pages will answer those questions.

FACT OR MYTH?

IS THE BIBLE REALLY "UNSCIENTIFIC"?

You will often hear that the Bible and science cannot agree, because (it is said) the very first proposition of the Bible[7], upon which the remainder of the book depends, is unproved and unprovable and therefore must be accepted by faith. By contrast, people think that science deals only with demonstrable and undeniable fact. Hence, they say, the factless faith of religion can be easily demolished by the faith-less *facts* of science. Or, we are told that science deals with objective truth, and practices common sense, while religion depends upon airy notions about the supernatural. We are asked to believe that science presents undeniable evidence, while religion has nothing stronger than subjective feelings. So science and the church are reckoned to be at war with each other.

Such claims are easy to disprove, for there are many ways in which scripture and science are equally dependent upon

---

[7] Genesis 1:1, "In the beginning God created the heavens and the earth."

"faith". They are different yet complementary aspects of the one great body of truth, and they share a similar cluster of suppositions. What those are will appear as this book unfolds; but let me begin by demonstrating that the idea of unassailable "fact" in science is a modern, and naive, prejudice. Indeed, when confronted with some of the claims made in the name of science, we might agree with the Red Queen -

> "I thought I'd try and find my way to the top of the hill" - Alice began to say.
>
> "When you say 'hill', the Queen interrupted, "*I* could show you hills, in comparison with which, you'd call that a valley."
>
> "No, I shouldn't," said Alice, surprised into contradicting her at last: "a hill **can't** be a valley, you know. That would be nonsense - "
>
> The Red Queen shook her head. "You may call it 'nonsense' if you like," she said, "but *I've* heard nonsense, compared with which that would be as sensible as a dictionary!"[8]

It would indeed be more sensible to call a hill a valley than to agree with the credulous assertion that science deals only with reality, and that it lacks any of the flimsy suppositions that many think are the basis of religion. Nowadays it is much truer to say that

> "The notion that the laws of science are permanently beyond question has to a large measure been replaced by the more ... skeptical view that all science is tentative. ... The laws of physics ... do not

---

[8] Lewis Carroll; Through the Looking Glass., chapter 2. But then the question may be, how sensible is a dictionary? At best, as Paul says, we are a people trying to see through clouded glass.

describe how nature goes on. They describe how the physicist goes on. ... Science then must not be regarded as cognitive, but rather as an attempt to utilise nature for our needs and wants ... Instead of being a gateway to all knowledge, science is not a way to any knowledge!"[9]

Many people, including some scientists, would gape at such sayings: *"The laws of physics describe how the physicist goes on ... Science is not a way to any knowledge!"* What does he mean? Simply that there are no real "laws" of nature. We only have definitions (which are constantly changing) invented by scientists to explain what is happening in their laboratories. But those definitions, and the way they are formed, are heavily influenced by the larger culture in which each scientist does his or her work. Therefore they really do say more about the practice of science than they have ever done about nature.[10]

"Perhaps that is true," you may be protesting; "but I still insist that science must be a way to discover truth. How can you say it is not a way to *any* knowledge?"

Well that depends upon what you mean by "knowledge". If you mean *information* that can be put to various uses in society, then science has obviously achieved splendid things. But if you mean *absolute* knowledge, truth that is unchangeable, a sure grasp upon final reality, the discovery of "why" rather than "what" or "how", *then science has nothing to say.* It is beset by limits it cannot overcome.[11]

---

[9] Professor Gordon H. Clark; from an article in Christianity Today, "Philosophy Of Science and Belief in God."

[10] See also para "Like A Recipe Book" below.

[11] I know the perils of such bold statements. See the Addendum at the end of this Chapter,"Never Say Never".

Those limits have been known since the Czech mathematician Curt Goedel (1906-1978) demonstrated that nothing in mathematics will ever be completely certain - which is an idea that most people still find astonishing. Surely, even if nothing else is certain, *mathematics* must deal with undeniable propositions? But Goedel showed that in any mathematical system there will always be contradictions, and that mathematics will always be plagued by paradoxes. No matter what system one constructs, questions remain that cannot be answered, mysteries that cannot be solved - at least, not from within the system itself. If any solution exists, it must be imported from outside the system, using rules and principles that are not part of that system.

Goedel's proofs were shattering to those mathematicians and physicists who had believed that the cosmos was a completely self-contained system, closed against any outside intervention (especially from some kind of god). One of their most basic beliefs had been that every problem must be solvable using only resources that lie within our reach. Some still believe that. But they can do so only by defying plain evidence to the contrary. The idea that interference from heaven in earthly affairs is scientifically impossible is a fallacy.

Goedel built his argument by showing first, that any truly consistent mathematical system must be complete within itself, containing nothing discontinuous, nothing self-contradictory, nothing left unresolved. Many mathematicians have struggled in vain to create just such a perfect, self-enclosed, entire system. Why have they been unable to do so? Because Goedel showed, second, that in any system formulae can be constructed that cannot be either proved or disproved from within that system. Then third, he demonstrated that no mathematical system can be proved to be consistent with its own rules without recourse to axioms[12] that exist only outside of that system.

Do those discoveries have any meaning for us? Yes, because when Goedel's Theorem of Incompleteness is applied to the larger environment, it shows that the earth will never be explained by using only the information contained in its own parts. The keys to a full explanation must finally come from outside the physical creation. Now that is good news for us Christians, for that is just what we have always said! Only when information is brought to us from outside can we hope to understand the world in which we live. Where shall we find such a report? Christians reply: in the pages of the Bible, in-breathed by the Holy Spirit. If someone chooses to deny the divine inspiration of scripture, then we can at least say this: no scientist working within the world can ever solve the deepest mysteries of the world. If God has not spoken, then we are condemned never to know.

A WORLD OF PARADOX

Because of the work of Goedel, and of others, scientists must now admit that from the point of view of rigorous logic, a paradox lies at the heart of the visible universe. An ancient puzzle illustrates what I mean -

> "Epimenides was a Cretan, who made one immortal statement, 'All Cretans are liars'[13] ... (That) is a statement that rudely violates the usually assumed dichotomy of statements into true and false, because if you tentatively think it is true, then it immediately backfires on you and makes you think it is false. But

---

[12] Here the word means a rule that must be accepted as true, without any further proof.

[13] See Tit 1:2.

once you've decided it is false, a similar backfiring returns you to the idea that it must be true. Try it!"[14]

Did you try it? If so, you found yourself puzzled by a statement that defies you to say whether it is true or false. But surely every statement *must* be one thing or the other? No, for we are facing a paradox (that is, logical spin-out, or inconsistency). It leads you into a dizzying circle, a baffling cycle of reasoning from which there is no escape![15] Many similar paradoxes can be constructed, for they are an inherent part of language and cannot be removed from it.[16]

Just as such logical, yet unresolvable, paradoxes are inseparable from the structure of any language, so they are also an integral part of everything that exists.

Now that is what Goedel displayed in his Theorem: paradox inexorably belongs to every imaginable mathematical system. Within them all propositions can be formulated for which the system itself provides no solution. Furthermore, propositions can be created that will be true in one system but false in another (or at least cannot be proved or disproved by a given system), while others may stand outside any conceivable system. As a consequence, early in this century

---

[14] Goedel, Escher, Bach, by Douglas Hofstadter; Vintage Books, NY, 1979; pg. 17.

[15] You may have noticed also that the only one who can finally tell if the statement is true or false is someone who is not a Cretan, who speaks from outside Crete. That is another reason why we, who are part of the world, cannot make any final pronouncement <u>about</u> the world. We must look to another source for the last word about ourselves! Christians, of course, find that source in the Word of God, the Bible.

[16] For more examples of paradox see the Addendum at the end of Chapter Four.

"mathematicians and philosophers had begun to have serious doubts about whether even the most concrete of theories, such as the study of whole numbers (1,2,3,4 ...) were built on solid foundations ... (Perhaps paradoxes) also exist in other branches of mathematics? Another related worry was that the paradoxes of logic, such as the Epimenides paradox, might turn out to be internal to mathematics, and thereby cast in doubt all of mathematics. This was especially worrisome to those - and there were a good number - who firmly believed that mathematics is simply a branch of logic (or conversely, that logic is simply a branch of mathematics)."[17]

When Alfred North Whitehead and Bertrand Russell wrote their *Principia Mathematica*[18] they made the same discovery. Their goal had been to reduce all mathematics to a logical certainty, so that nothing irrational or uncertain remained.[19] Instead they had to face the bleak reality that

---

[17] Hofstadter, op cit. Pg. 23.

[18] The Principia Mathematica was possibly the greatest and most rigorously intellectual work ever written on this theme, or perhaps any other. The authors attempted to describe a mathematical system that was (1) consistent (that is free of any contradiction) and (2) complete (that is, every true statement can be derived from within its own framework). They failed.

[19] In one volume they devoted 362 pages to proving that 1+1=2. That too was in vain. Mathematicians now know that even the most basic equations may be true only within a particular system. In another system, with a different environment, different parameters, different rules, the equation may become 1+1=n (where n is a number other than 2). Nothing in the world is certain - except God! For another approach to this puzzle see the last of the Paradoxes that are listed in the Addendum that follows Chapter Four.

> "(Goedel's 1931 paper) revealed not only that there were irreparable 'holes' in the axiomatic system proposed by Russell and Whitehead, but more generally that *no* axiomatic system whatsoever could produce all number-theoretical truths, unless it were an inconsistent system ... (All) hope of proving the consistency of a system such as that presented in 'P. M.' was shown to be vain ... "[20]

Russell and Whitehead were obliged to accept that their colossal and brilliant labour had been futile, so that Russell later wrote -

> "I wanted certainty in the kind of way in which people want religious faith. I thought that certainty is more likely to be found in mathematics than elsewhere. But after some twenty years of arduous toil, I came to the conclusion that there was nothing more that I could do."[21]

Hence Professor Michael Atiyah of Oxford University once confessed -

> "Most working mathematicians take a pragmatic attitude. If we can't achieve ultimate certainty about maths, by providing foundations, that is no reason for us to stop doing mathematics. Physicists get along quite happily even though *their foundations are much shakier than ours!*"[22]

Now there's an illuminating comment! Here is a mathematician acknowledging the murky foundations upon

---

[20] Paradigms Lost, by John L. Casti; William Morrow & Co, N.Y., 1989; pg. 24.

[21] I have lost the source of that quote, as well as of the one following.

[22] Emphasis mine

which his discipline is built. Then he justifies it by declaring that physics stands upon a still more wobbly footing!

If you are unaware of what is happening in the world of science you will probably find such statements almost unbelievable. All your life you may have been taught that mathematics and physics rely only upon the hardest verifiable evidence, so that their findings are sure and dependable. Of course, at a certain pragmatic level, that is true, otherwise our civilization would long since have collapsed into chaos. Nonetheless, the findings of science, while they do produce much useful knowledge, remain true only within definite boundaries. Beyond those walls, and underlying the whole structure, is a vast expanse of uncertainty. The foundations of science ultimately stand upon a swamp of foggy paradox and impenetrable mystery.[23]

We are like a child with a set of coloured blocks. At first he scatters them carelessly, but he will eventually begin to make some sense out of them and gain some use from them. He may build a tower, a bridge, a fortress; he will assemble the pieces in ways that bring him pleasure and benefit. But in the end he knows no more about the actual origin of his blocks, nor about their real nature, than when he began. He doesn't even know whether he has put them together in the worst way or the best. He will develop some guiding principles on how to handle coloured blocks; but he cannot tell whether or not a different set of principles would have served him better. That is what science is like; those are the limits within which science must work.

---

[23] Rather like the building in which you are probably sitting as you read these words. Its foundation seems secure enough. Yet you know that (in comparison with the size of the Earth), you need only dig down a short distance and you will find molten rock.

NO FIRM RULES

Paul Feyerband, in his manifesto "Against Method", argues that

> "no set of rules can ever be found to guide the scientist in his choice of theories, and to imagine that there is such is to impede progress ... "

Do you understand what that means? Simply that what is often today called the reliable "scientific method" is just one tradition chosen out of many possible tracks. Clever people in our society "do" science in a way that is acceptable to their peers; but they cannot know whether or not they are doing it in the best way, or whether or not a different set of theorems might have brought better results. Their discoveries may work well enough. They may be immensely useful to humanity. Yet they may relate to real truth no more closely than a child's sand castle does to a majestic cathedral. The honest scientist will admit that

> "there are many ways of coming to scientific truth, and what is taken to be true at any moment is more a matter of social convention in the scientific community than it is the product of logical methods and procedures."[24]

LIKE A RECIPE-BOOK

Unhappily (like those three wise men of Gotham), many scientists are strongly committed to the basic assumptions that underlie their theorems. So they routinely find ways to explain away, or simply ignore, the many anomalies they encounter. They can be obliged to abandon their assumptions (as the history of science shows) only under extreme pressure. But honest scholars are acknowledging with humility that

---

[24] Casti, op. Cit. Pg 38.

"(Science proceeds on the assumption) that everything can be reduced to established facts or hypotheses. But in fact, reality itself is a hypothesis. *Science is a collection of successful recipes.* Science proceeds more by what it has learned to ignore than what it takes into account. You never solve problems. You just move on to new problems!"[25]

"Science is a collection of successful recipes." What an arresting observation! It is a variation on the illustration above about a child's building blocks, except that now we are in a kitchen. On the shelf stands a host of ingredients. How will the chef blend them? What an infinite variety of choices he can make! We trust he will choose well, bake truly, and produce a fine dish. Yet how can he ever know if he has created the best possible dish? Furthermore, the meals he does prepare will be as much fixed by the palates of his customers as by the possibilities inherent in the ingredients. Even the items he has on his shelves will be determined by the wants of his diners. Some foods that are hailed in other lands are never likely to appear on his menu!

Scientists must make similar choices, and they are governed by similar prejudices. The supposed objectivity and neutrality of science is a myth.

BELIEVING IS SEEING

The previous quote contained another startling sentence: "Reality itself is a hypothesis." Here is one of the most vexed questions in modern physics: what is the connection between the theories of a scientist and the objective reality he is trying to explain?

---

[25] Remarks made at a National Home Study Council seminar by Dr. E. K. Young, of the National University, Washington. Emphasis mine.

> realists argue that objective reality does exist; whether or not anyone sees the Earth, the planets, and all, makes no difference; they are truly there.

> relativists argue that reality is what the community says it is, and this differs from time to time, and from place to place..

I will be coming back to this question, What is reality?[26] For now just notice that there is no indisputable way to prove that anything we see actually exists. We are, of course, obliged to assume that what we perceive at least approximates the true state of things! We take it for granted that our perceptions are fairly reliable. Yet in the end the only proof we have is statistical. Because everybody around us apparently sees the same things, we conclude that the messages sent to us by our five senses are trustworthy.

But now walk into a hospital for the insane. There you will find many people who seem quite healthy, yet their perceptions of the world differ radically from yours! To them, their world is as real as yours is to you. The main reason they are locked up while you and I walk free is because there are more of us than there are of them! Yet you can no more prove *objectively*[27] that *your* perceptions represent truth than they can.

Consider also this striking statement by Professor Owen Gingerich -

> "Today in science there is no 'belief' as such, only probability. As an example, physicists, if pressed,

---

[26] Mainly in Chapter Four and in the Addendum that follows it.

[27] That is, rationally, dispassionately, using the canons of science. Statistical proof is not finally "scientific" proof. Not that that is a problem, because science never can "prove" anything according to its own rules.

will say that atoms, as real objects in the form in which we imagine them, cannot be proved. The most you can say is that the universe behaves as if it were made of atoms. With the stars, too, we know the stars only as grains of light exposed on photographic plates. Proof of what they are is absent. Astronomic knowledge may be highly probable, but it cannot be asserted to be absolutely true. In practice, scientists ignore this, and behave as though they were dealing with undeniable fact. But if pressed, they will admit that belief in absolute reality collapsed just after the turn of the century, with Einstein. Time itself proved to be elastic, a matter of perception. Matter proved to be fluid and quirky. Much of the absolute reality of time and space had to be abandoned. It became apparent that no measurement is absolute[28]. Since then, one simply cannot speak of certainties, but only of probabilities."[29]

---

[28] No two people can ever make <u>exactly</u> the same measurement; nor can one person ever <u>exactly</u> repeat a measurement. A slightly different result will be obtained every time. The barrier seems to be not so much physical as metaphysical as; more related to philosophy than to physics, yet with an unavoidable effect upon the physical dimension.

[29] Based on remarks made at a Washington symposium in 1982, Professor Gingerich, an astronomer from Harvard University and from the Smithsonian Astrophysical Observatory, caused quite a stir by his remarks. Many in the audience were disturbed to learn that their "certainties" were no longer certain!
Note: on the question of atoms; scientists have "seen" atoms and electrons only in the trails they leave in bubble chambers, or in the form of greatly enlarged shadows produced in an electron microscope. But suppose we had no evidence of fireworks rockets except trails in the night sky, or occasional photographs of their explosions. and then had to deduce what they were!

On another occasion Dr. Gingerich also said -

> "It is an irony of history that Galileo's own methods of scientific argument (by which he had hoped to bring certainty out of confusion) were instrumental in showing that what passes for truth in science is only the likely or the probable; truth can never be final, never absolute ... It is this process that the poet Robinson Jeffers had in mind when he wrote: 'The mathematicians and the physics men have their mythology; they work alongside the truth, never touching it; their equations are false, but the things work.'
>
> "The mathematicians and the physicists cannot really claim truth, but they have certainly sorted out a lot of things that do not work, and they are building a wondrously coherent picture of the universe."[30]

Note again the significant comment: *"Scientific knowledge may be highly probable, but it cannot be asserted to be absolutely true."* That is, proof is lacking from a strictly scientific point of view - which depends (or should depend) upon empirical evidence, not theory. Yet we all assume the truth of the reality that surrounds us. This assumption is an act of faith. Which leads on to the surprising discovery that all scientific endeavour begins with an act of faith - but further exploration of that idea will have to wait for the next chapter. Let me now close this one with a paragraph about the great Scottish social commentator, Thomas Carlyle, who 150 years ago saw the logical and spiritual dilemma science was already beginning to fall into -

---

[30] From an article "The Galileo Affair", in the "Scientific American", August 1982.

"The science of Carlyle's time was busy proclaiming that, since the universe is governed by natural laws, miracles are impossible and the supernatural is a myth. Carlyle replies that the natural laws are themselves only manifestations of Spiritual Forces, and that thus miracle is everywhere and all nature supernatural. We, who are the creatures of time and space, can indeed apprehend the Absolute only when he weaves about him the visible garments of time and space. Thus God reveals himself to sense through symbols. But it is as we regard these symbols in one or other of two possible ways that we class ourselves with the foolish or with the wise. The foolish man sees only the symbol, thinks it exists for itself, takes it for ultimate fact, and therefore rests in it. The wise man sees the symbol, knows it is only a symbol, and penetrates into it for the ultimate fact or spiritual reality which it symbolises."[31]

---

[31] From the "Introduction" by William H. Hudson to "Sartor Resartus"; J. M. Dent & Sons, London, 1913; pg.xiii.

28

ADDENDUM

NEVER SAY NEVER

I am aware of the danger of saying that something can "never" be done. History is littered with a trail of discarded pronouncements about something being "impossible", which someone then turned around and did. Here are a couple of examples from T. H. White's fascinating exploration of English upper-class life in the late 18th century. In the first, Boswell reports the comments of his friend Dr Johnson on "the possible speeds of earlier days" -

> "The English (said he) are the only people who ride hard a-hunting. A Frenchman goes out upon a managed horse, and capers in the field, and no more thinks of leaping a hedge than of mounting a breach. Lord Powerscourt laid a wager, in France, that he would ride a great many miles in a certain short time. The French academicians set to work, and calculated that, from the resistance of the air, it was impossible. His lordship, however, performed it."[32]

Then in 1829, a gentleman named Creevey had his first train ride, which he described thus -

> "I had the satisfaction, for I can't call it pleasure, of taking a trip of five miles in it, which we did in just a quarter of an hour - that is, twenty miles an hour. ... But observe, during these five miles, the machine was occasionally made to put itself out or *go* it; and then we went at the rate of 23 miles an hour .... But the quickest motion is to me *frightful* ... It gave me a

---

[32] The Age of Scandal; The Folio Society, London. 1993; pg 30.

headache which has not left me yet. Sefton is convinced that some damnable thing must come of it!"

I give you those quotes only because I happened to read White's book while I was writing this one. It would not be difficult to add a score of similar examples of prejudice and ignorance. Countless past scientific "certainties" have been turned into nonsense. Nonetheless, there does seem to be a more firmly rational basis for the admissions that are now being made about the limitations of science. In some of the realms discussed above, there truly does seem to be a real barrier to any absolute achievement in knowledge. Nor is the barrier merely physical; it is metaphysical in character - a philosophical, or better, a spiritual wall. In the reckoning of a growing number of scientists a point has already been reached where some of the discoveries of the laboratory must yield to the revelation of scripture.

Chapter Two

UNPROVABLE ASSUMPTIONS

"But is not a real Miracle simply a violation of the Laws of nature?" ask several. Whom I answer by this new question: What are the Laws of Nature? To me perhaps the rising of one from the dead were no violation of these Laws, but a confirmation (were I able to understand) of some far deeper Law ...

"But is it not the deepest Law of Nature that she be constant?" cries an illuminated class: "is not the Machine of the Universe[33] fixed to move by unalterable rules?" Probable enough, good friends; nay I, too, must believe that the God, whom ancient inspired men assert to be 'without variableness or shadow of turning', does indeed never change; that Nature, that the Universe, which no one whom it so pleases can be prevented from calling a Machine, does move by the most unalterable rules. And now of you, too, I make the old enquiry: What those same unalterable rules, forming the complete Statute-book of nature, may possibly be?

"They stand written in our Works of Science," say you; "in the accumulated records of Man's Experience!" - Was Man with his Experience present at the Creation, then, to see how it all went on? Have any deepest scientific individuals yet dived-down to the foundations of the Universe, and gauged

---

[33] This was the predominant view, now heavily modified, of 19th century science.

everything there? Did the Maker take them into his counsel; that they read his ground plan of the incomprehensible All; and can say, This stands marked therein, and no more than this? Alas, not in anywise! These scientific individuals have been nowhere but where we also are; have seen some handbreadths deeper than we see into the Deep that is infinite, without bottom as without shore. ...

"System of Nature! To the wisest man, wide as is his vision, Nature remains of quite *infinite* depth, of quite infinite expansion; and all Experience thereof limits itself to some few computed centuries and measured square-miles. ... To the Minnow, every cranny and pebble, and quality and accident, of its little native Creek may have become familiar; but does the Minnow understand the Ocean Tides and periodic Currents, the Trade-winds and Monsoons, and Moon's Eclipses; by all which the condition of its little Creek is regulated, and may, from time to time (*un*-miraculously enough), be quite overset and reversed? Such a minnow is Man; his Creek this Planet Earth; his Ocean the immeasurable All; his Monsoons and periodic Currents the Mysterious Course of Providence through Aeons and Aeons."[34]

How prescient Carlyle was! The developments of modern science, far from outdating and invalidating his argument, have given it more strength than ever. Recent discoveries in Chaos Theory, and in Quantum Mechanics[35], have shown us how little we actually *know*, and what an awesome foundation of mystery undergirds the world we see around us. The whole scientific edifice stands, not upon a sure

---

[34] Thomas Carlyle, op. cit., Book Three, Chapter Eight, "Natural Supernaturalism"; pg. 192, 193.

[35] Which I will return to later.

foundation of objective fact, but upon a series of impenetrable postulates. Here then is something that all scientists know, yet seldom think about, and even more rarely state openly: **all scientific research depends upon assumptions that are both unproved and unprovable.** This chapter and the next explore some of those assumptions. The first is

THE UNIFORMITY OF NATURE

"What I assume, you shall assume."[36]

The basic assumption upon which all rational thought about the world is based is an idea called "the uniformity of nature". It holds that *nature is uniform in all its parts.* No matter where in the universe you may travel, you will find there the same natural laws. Throughout the cosmos everything is subject to the same physical and chemical constraints. For example, we assume that the law of gravity works in England just as it does in Australia. But the scientist also assumes that it works the same way on every planet in our solar system, and throughout the galaxy, and in every galaxy across the entire universe.

Three accessories to this idea are

- nature is "good", and will yield her secrets and benefits to diligent research;
- "progress" is inherent in the scheme of things; and
- increased knowledge will lead to the betterment of human life.

Yet those propositions must all be called "assumptions" - that is, they are not susceptible to any formal or final proof.

---

[36] Walt Whitman, American poet (1819-1892); from "Song of Myself".

Sir Isaac Newton (1642-1727), of falling-apple fame, helped to lay the foundations of modern scientific research by his use of an early form of the principle of natural uniformity. Having been driven out of London by the plague, Newton was meditating one day in the orchard of his mother's country home, when an apple fell onto his head. At that moment he had been pondering why the moon kept its orbit so faithfully. The accident caused him to wonder if the force that pulled an apple down might also be the one that kept the planets and stars in their places in the sky. His reflections led him to develop the mechanics of motion, both terrestrial and celestial. Order and reason were at once brought into the study of astronomy. A reliable basis was provided for the scientific development that has continued unabated from then until now.[37]

One of Newton's rules was: "The qualities of bodies within the reach of our experiments are to be deemed the universal qualities of all bodies." That is to say: sensible thought about the universe is impossible unless one takes it for granted (without proof) that a piece of rock in the distant galaxy of Andromeda will behave in the same way as a piece of rock on our planet. But without going to Andromeda, how can anyone actually *prove* Newton's rule?

When I was at high school the science teacher demonstrated the use of a spectroscope. A beam of light was shone through a prism onto a white screen, where it produced an array of coloured bands - all the colours of the "rainbow"[38]. We learnt that each strip of colour represented a natural element, and

---

[37] Newton himself saw in his discoveries strong evidence of the reality of God, who is the uniform Creator, not only of all that exists, but also of the laws that govern the workings of nature throughout the entire universe. In fact, he wrote more books on Christian doctrine than he did on science!

[38] Which of course is itself caused by rain drops acting like tiny prisms

that by analysing the spectral graphs of various stars the physical constituency of each one could be determined. The experiment, of course, was meaningful only if one assumed that a ray of light from a distant star could be interpreted in the same way as a ray of light from the earth. As Albert Einstein once said, "Without a belief in the inner harmony of the world, there could be no science."[39]

Notice how Einstein used the term "belief". One must *believe* in the "inner harmony of the world", because there is no conceivable way of "proving" it. The uniformity of nature is a "truth" that we must accept without demonstration. Why? Simply because "proof" would require someone to travel to every single spot in the universe and there perform the same set of experiments. Even then, the "proof" would remain only statistical, not absolute. That is, it would be based neither upon pure unassailable reason, nor upon incontestable demonstration, but only upon a large number of repetitions. Those repetitions may create a high level of probability, but the final conclusion must remain open to question.

The Austrian philosopher Ludwig Wittgenstein (1889-1951) realised the uncertainty that lies at the heart of everything we think has been "proved". So he propounded a theory, which is now widely accepted: all the rules of logic we accept without question are based merely upon a lifelong community consensus. He meant that there are no fundamental rules of the sort that any group of intelligent people, working apart from each other, free from any cultural conditioning, would arrive at independently. Our "rules" and axioms all arise out of, and belong to, the social group of which we happen to be members.

---

[39] Quoted by C. A. Patrides, in his "Introduction" to Sir Thomas Browne - The Major Works; Penguin Books, 1977; pg. 36.

> "The implications of all this for science is that science rests upon a foundation of taken-for-granted realities..."[40]

But if those "realities" are "taken-for-granted" then we are talking about a set of ideas that the community has simply agreed to accept as true, without any logical proof or demonstration. Is there any reason why we should do this? And what is the origin of the particular assumption we are looking at here, "the uniformity of nature"? And how can it be assumed that nature is "good", or that "progress" is inevitable? None of those ideas are in any way self-evident. They are simply assumed, without any necessary logical reason to do so. Why then do we assume them?

A LEGACY OF THE REFORMATION

The idea that natural law is everywhere in the universe the same was first presented by the English Scholastic philosopher William of Ockham (1290-1349).[41] He held that nearly every proposition natural science could present is unavoidably based, not upon pure reason, but upon practical experience. From the results of various experiments, certain conclusions are reached. But then comes the question: how can one take those results out of the laboratory and put them to use in the world? Answer: only by conjecturing that a set of rules exists which control natural behaviour - not just in the laboratory, but everywhere. If such rules do not exist, then one can never be sure that the experiment will work a second time. But then comes another question: whence came those stabilising rules? According to Ockham, the

---

[40] Casti, op.cit., pg. 31.
[41] See also the next chapter, under the Fourth Assumption, "The Simplest Explanation is the Best."

answer to that question leads irresistibly to God. [42] In any case, his ideas were among the first gleams of the modern "scientific method" to shine into the intellectual darkness of mediaeval Europe.

The principles Ockham had suggested were taken up with special vigour by the Protestant Reformers in the 16th century and after. They forcibly broke away from ancient superstitions and mediaeval mysticism, and submitted every part of their lives and thought to scripture. They rediscovered the biblical idea that God is rational, and that the universe has been built with order and purpose. They grasped in a different way the original biblical mandate to *"occupy the earth, take authority over it."* A new age dawned, and a new way of thinking flourished. The earth became a resource to develop for the glory of God.

> "About 350 years ago there was a significant advance in the growth and development of science. It occurred in the West, as every historian knows. It flowed on from the Renaissance, and was inseparable from the factors that led to the Reformation. While it is perhaps too difficult to pinpoint all of the reasons for the remarkable leap forward at that time, historians of science would all agree that men realised for the first time that they were studying a measurable and predictable world ... Why did this happen in the West? Because the Bible was known. Because men were liberated from superstition and from the capricious, because the view taken of the universe was the biblical view.
>
> "A great French philosopher wrote at this time: Without God a man could not trust in anything, could

---

[42] His main purpose in developing the principle was actually not scientific but theological.

not believe in a geometrical proposition, for he is the guarantee that everyone is not an illusion, the senses not a complete hoax, and life not a mere nightmare ...

"Ultimately we are dealing with truth. There is more evidence for the resurrection of Christ than there is for the existence of the Roman Empire! ... Science grew as a discipline of truth in a biblical culture, and the God of the Book is the God revealed in Jesus Christ[43]" ...

That letter echoes another idea that William of Ockham propounded: God has established two different orders, one of *nature* and one of *grace*:

- ➢ nowadays we learn about the *order of nature* by experience, and gain benefit from it by using the principle of natural uniformity, which enables us to apply our experiences to life everywhere;
- ➢ but, like Ockham, we too must admit that we can learn about the *order of grace* only by revelation, which comes to us through the scriptures.

So God has given us two books: one the Book of Nature; the other the Holy Bible. Those books must be read differently, but they are not in conflict with each other. The scientist and the theologian may work independently, but they should both remain submissive to and dependent upon the will of God, for they are pursuers together of the truth of God.[44]

---

[43] Dr Kenneth O. Goodwin, principal research scientist at the CSIRO, Australia, in a letter to the Adelaide Advertiser, c. 1980.

[44] Information about William of Ockham from the Dictionary of Philosophy and Religion, ed. W. L. Reese; Harvester Press, Sussex; 1980.

THE GREEKS AND THE ROMANS

Here then is a piece of history that you may find surprising: *belief in a rational universe is unique to Christian civilisation*. Why? Because it cannot arise where the universe is thought to be erratic, controlled by warring and unpredictable deities. Science is impossible when people think either that nature herself is capricious, or that she is controlled by aberrant forces. Yet that is just what most people throughout history *have* believed!

Because you and I have been brought up in a culture profoundly committed to the idea of predictable natural law, we find it difficult to realise how few people have ever thought that way. Yet in this matter we represent a small minority of humanity. Across history the vast majority of people have never doubted that nature is altogether mysterious, and her behaviour hazardous and capricious.

For example, consider the ancient Greeks and Romans. They were rational people, their achievements were brilliant, and the greatest minds among them (Socrates, Plato, Aristotle) were every bit equal to the finest intellects of our own time. Therefore you may think they viewed the world much the same as we do. Why then did the scientific method arise only recently in the West, and never in Greece or Rome? Or in Egypt, or China? Simply because not even the wisest among the ancients ever saw the world as you and I see it. How could they, when they worshipped a multitude of deities and demi-gods, who were thought to control every aspect of life? Augustine (354-430), for example, described the absurdity of Roman religion -

> "But how can I give a list, in one passage of this book, of all the names of their gods and goddesses? The Romans had difficulty in getting them into the massive volumes in which they assigned particular

functions and special responsibilities to the various divine powers."[45]

Then Augustine gives a long list of deities (which he adds to elsewhere in his book), and he details the particular responsibility assigned to each god or goddess. Among the items of daily life that each had their own ruling deity were:

- plains; hills; valleys; crops; seed just sown; shoots appearing above the ground; germinating corn; ears of corn; harvested grain; stored produce; houses; doorsteps; doors; windows; trees; lakes; rivers; clouds; rain; human intercourse; conception; parturition; lactation; eating; drinking; sleeping; awaking; labour; pleasure; gold; silver; war; peace
- indeed, almost every aspect of personal, domestic, community, and national life you could think of!

In many cases, one higher god had general authority over an object, but under him were numerous lesser deities, who cared for its various parts. Augustine sums up the whole idolatrous panoply in several splendidly sarcastic passages, of which I will here quote just one. In it he describes the numerous gods and goddesses required to supervise just one thing, the growth of an ear of corn -

> "Would not anyone think that Segetia would have been competent to supervise the whole process from the first green shoots to the dry ears of corn? But that was not enough for men who loved a multitude of gods - and so much so that their miserable soul disdained the pure embrace of the one true God and

---

[45] City of God Book IV, ch. 9; tr. Henry Bettenson; ed. David Knowles; Penguin Books, London, 1977.

prostituted itself to a multitude of demons. So they put Proserpina in command of germinating corn; the god Nodutus looked after the nodes and joints on the stalks; the goddess Voluntina saw to the envelopes of the follicles; when the follicles opened to release the spike, the goddess Patelana took over; when the crops were evenly eared, then came the turn of the goddess Hostilina; when the crops were blooming, the goddess Flora came in; when they became milky, the god Lacturnus; when they were maturing, the goddess Matuta; when they were plucked up, the goddess Runcina."[46]

All those deities had to be placated and persuaded just to get a good ear of corn! Nigel Lambourne sums it up by saying,

"(Since the Romans) were a race of farmers, every act and process of the agricultural life had its protective *numen*[47], who had to be treated with proper respect."[48]

Similarly, R. M. Ogilvie describes the chaotic superstition of Roman religion -

"(Most) of the things which were vital for the wellbeing of society were thought of as functions of a god or as gods functioning. A house is only as secure as its door: the opening and closing of the door, and the passage of a man from the privacy of his home into the racket of the outside world, and vice versa, can be critical events, and in consequence they were held to be in the power of a god, Janus. Janus

---

[46] Ibid. See also Bk. IV.23; Bk. VI.9; and numerous other statements scattered throughout the "City of God".

[47] In Roman mythology, a presiding demon, divinity, or spirit.

[48] From the "Introduction" to his translation of Virgil's The Georgics; Folio Society, London, 1969; pg. 10.

Patulcius opened the door, Janus Clusivius closed it. Whether the opening and closing resulted in good or evil for the person concerned would, therefore depend on Janus' favour. ... (other gods presided over the threshold, the door hinges, and the door leaf) ...

"Particularly in a farming community, the sky and the changing pattern of the weather command constant attention. The sun has appeared for the last thousand days: is it certain that it will appear tomorrow? How does it operate, and how is it controlled? ... How is rain rationed? The terrifying and unpredictable flashes of lightning contain huge stores of energy. How are they directed? ... With poor communications and dangerous roads it would be a rash thing to set out on a journey without having squared 'the god who invented roads and paths'."[49]

You should notice two things here -

1. A Sensible View

Your first response to such ignorant superstitions may be one of scorn. But don't be too hasty. The opinion of the ancients is in some respects more rational than ours, for the vicissitudes of life (even in the modern world) do indeed suggest that heaven is fickle and hateful rather than benign and dependable. Floods and famines, fires and earthquakes, pestilence and drought, seem to alternate with peace, prosperity, and wellbeing, without any observable purpose or pattern. One part of the land bakes under a burning sun while another is ravaged by wildly swirling water. Plague sweeps through a community, destroying this family and

---

[49] The Romans and Their Gods; W. W. Norton and Co, New York, 1969; pg. 11, 12.

that, yet leaving many untouched. Millions of ordinary people endure unending poverty, a prison of misery from which they cannot hope to escape. Every year tens of thousands of children perish from starvation, or die exhausted by hard labour before they reach adolescence. How often the wicked amass wealth, while the virtuous are crushed! Good falls upon the evil and evil upon the good; life's rewards seem cruelly inequitable. Without the revelation of scripture, and apart from faith, it is not easy to discern in the changing fortunes of each day the guiding hand of the benevolent Father.[50]

Because our society has a deeply Christian background, and against the daily evidence of its own TV screens, our community continues to believe that the world is rational and ultimately good. Even those who have rejected the Christian faith unconsciously cling to this Christian world-view. Yet once the Bible is scorned, what ground remains for anyone to sustain such a belief? Not because of but *against* reason people cling to their trust in nature's benevolence. Yet surely the most undaunted optimist who looks across the earth, who sees the pain of countless millions and hears their helpless cry, must fall into despair -

> I held it truth, with him who sings
> To one clear harp in divers tones,
> That men may rise on stepping-stones
> Of their dead selves to higher things.

---

[50] At first sight, the above comments may seem to contradict the scriptures quoted in Chapter One, which say that God's eternal power and glory can be clearly seen in the things he has made. That witness remains strong and should be enough to convince anyone who looks at the wonders of creation. Nonetheless, under the impact of powerful superstitions, added to the awful impact of sin upon both humanity and the physical creation (Ge 3:17-19), most men and women throughout history have been rendered blind (Ro 1:21-22; Ep 4:18-19; 2 Co 4:4).

> But who shall so forecast the years,
> And find in loss a gain to match?
> Or reach a hand thro' time to catch
> The far-off interest of tears?
>
> O sorrow, cruel fellowship,
> O Priestess in the vaults of Death,
> O sweet and bitter in a breath,
> What whispers from thy lying lip?
>
> "The stars," she whispers, "blindly run:
> A web is wov'n across the sky;
> From out waste places comes a cry,
> And murmurs from the dying sun:
>
> "And all the phantom, Nature, stands -
> With all the music in her tone,
> A hollow echo of my own -
> A hollow form with empty hands."[51]

Aside from the good news of the gospel, how could any honest observer quarrel with the poet's gloomy verdict? The stars surely do run blindly, without purpose across the heavens. Nature is nothing better than a hollow form with hollow hands, mindless, dumb, lacking destiny, drained of value. And we who dwell here are but specks of dust, phantom echoes of a decaying world. Even the superstitions of the ancients are preferable to such utter bleakness!

---

[51] Alfred, Lord Tennyson, "In Memorium" (1850); I.1,2 and III.1,2,3. After 132 sections of various length, Tennyson ends his epic poem with a cry that nothing is left but faith in God. Yet it is a faith built upon despair rather than upon faith. Truly, in the face of the world's infinite sorrow it does indeed take a clear perception of scripture not to hold that lamentation is more reasonable than laughter.

2. *Frightening Cosmos*

Consider now the impossibility of anything like modern science developing under the rule of the Caesars. When every event of every day is controlled by a vast array of divinities, all of whom must be humoured, how can anyone be certain of the outcome of any action? When the favour of a thousand deities must be constantly bought by sacrifices and prayer, how can anyone be sure even of today, let alone tomorrow? When nothing can happen unless the ruling god permits it, nothing can be depended upon - not even tomorrow's sunrise, or next season's harvest, or anything else in the world.

The Romans did not live in a world governed by immutable natural law, impersonal and dependable, but in a world haunted by a host of gods and demi-gods. The fate of each day was fixed by a multitude of demons both good and bad, and by a horde of other preternatural beings and forces.

No Roman army marched until the heavens gave a favourable sign; no great enterprise was begun unless the augurs spoke well; the destiny of the state was thought not to be in the hands of its citizens but in the caprice of the mischievous inhabitants of the skies.

When he opened his door, a devout Roman breathed a prayer to the god who controlled the open door, and another to the threshold deity as he crossed over the step, and yet another to the ruler of closing doors as he passed through the portal, and a prayer again as he stepped onto the footpath, and so on, and on, and on. He did this with hardly any thought, simply as part of his daily routine. But his practice inevitably shaped his world-view, immersing him in superstition, preventing him from thinking sensibly about the world around him.

Nor were scholars and thinkers (even when they mocked the worst of the pagan myths) immune from such an all-pervasive influence. They too were effectively blocked from developing what today would be called "the scientific method". The result was that research as we understand it was never begun. What is the point of conducting an experiment in a laboratory when its outcome may depend entirely upon the caprice of some spiteful goddess?

That is why the Greeks focused their brilliance upon abstract thought and upon the arts. They pondered the interior life of the soul, but avoided any detailed analysis of the physical environment. The Romans expended their energies on law, government, and empire - the earth was too sacrosanct to be dissected. Pharaoh devoted the resources of Egypt to the massive demands of an all-pervading religion. Each of the ancient peoples were blocked by superstition from looking at the world, or treating it, as we do.

Throughout history, and into the modern world, virtually all cultures have held to a worldview similar to that of the ancient Greeks and Romans[52]. The main, if not the only, exceptions have been those nations heavily influenced first by the 15th century Renaissance, and then more strongly by the 16th century Reformation. But why did those two events lead to modern science? Because out of them arose two things that are necessary for the development of a "scientific" method.[53] Those two things are: a *stable society*; and a *sound philosophical base*. Now both of those came into

---

[52] See the Addendum at the end of this chapter for an example of how even in England, right up until the time of the Reformation, the advance of learning was hobbled by superstition. Even after the Reformation a hundred years had to pass before investigators and inventors could feel free to pursue their studies wherever they might lead. It took several generations to percolate the new worldview through all levels of society, and finally break the strong arm of superstition.

[53] The ancients concentrated on pragmatic skills, such as building construction, pottery, metal-working, and the like.

existence in Europe during the Middle Ages, and reached their flower by the end of the Reformation period. But one or the other of them was lacking from ancient societies (and are still lacking from many modern ones).

For example, ancient Egypt enjoyed some 30 centuries of unbroken identity - the longest span of social continuity in human history. No other culture has equaled the enduring stability nor the lasting peace and prosperity enjoyed by the subjects of Pharaoh. Yet they produced nothing resembling what we call "science". Why were they so unproductive? Simply because they had the first requirement for scientific development (a stable society), but not the second (an adequate philosophy). Their culture was tightly interwoven with a complex web of superstition that reached from the throne to the peasant's stool. So they had an altogether unsuitable philosophical and religious base upon which to build an edifice of research and scientific development.

There was a further problem. Many ancient and modern cultures have seen the world itself as a living thing. Sometimes like a wild animal, whose actions were unpredictable. Sometimes as a goddess whose co-operation must be sought. Sometimes as the manifestation of some deity, whom it is fatal to offend. The uncertainty and inconsistency of such a worldview is shown by the shape of their idols: hybrid mixtures of birds, animals, humans, and bizarre mythological creatures. The stone figures reveal the uncertainty of the worshippers: is their god animal, or human, or earthly, or heavenly? Holding such a twisted purview how could any society develop any consistency of thought? But the changes that swept over Europe during the 15th and 16th centuries transformed all this -

> "Many reasons, of course, have been put forward to account for the flourishing of science in 16th-century Europe and, more particularly, in 17th-century England: a Protestant ethic or ethos wedded to the

needs of a nascent capitalism; the navigating practicalities of a maritime nation; the recent availability of a simple technology ...

"But much of the engine power for the development of modern science undoubtedly stemmed from the conceptual revolution engendered by the rediscovery of a biblical attitude to the natural milieu, an attitude almost lost through mediaeval theology's tendency to mystify nature by all but conflating Creator and creation.

"In rediscovering the contingency of the natural order - separated in essence from God and yet dependent upon him for its ultimate being and inherent structure - scientists now had a philosophical imprimatur for the assurance that the secrets of the natural world could be discovered by empirical observation, and by observation alone."[54]

The church re-discovered the New Testament revelation of Christ as the eternal Logos, through whom, by whom, and for whom the universe and all it contains was created (Cl 1:15-19). Out of this came a renewed sense of order and purpose in the universe. The belief became dominant that a rational God would not create an irrational world, that a law-keeping God could not make a lawless earth. Suddenly, two ideas could be accepted that would have seemed absurd to ancient cultures: the world is *rational*; and it is *contingent*.[55] If it is *rational*, then the reason for things can be sought and found; if it is *contingent*, then we have a duty to go out and discover how better to fulfil God's purpose in it. As someone

---

[54] David N. Livingstone, Evolution As Metaphor and Myth, in the Christian Scholar's Review Vol. 12, #2, 1983.

[55] "Contingent" in this setting means created by God, and dependent upon him for its continuance and proper functioning.

has said: "If the world is not rational, science is not possible; if it is not contingent, science is not necessary."

So in Europe old superstitions began to crumble. The new certainties that scholars were reaching in sacred knowledge led to confidence that the same certainties could be gained in secular knowledge. If God is revealing ever more of himself through the *Word,* then he must also be willing to reveal himself through the *World.* Every nation affected by the Renaissance and the Reformation felt a massive shift in the way people looked at their surroundings. A culture that had never before existed was created. In this wonderful new world modern science could be born and flourish.

WHAT ABOUT ISRAEL?

I am sure that at least some readers are ready to object: "But what about Israel? Was their view of nature not the same as ours? Why did they not develop a culture of science?"

Ancient Israel in fact lacked both of the elements needed to create an environment favourable to scientific discovery: a stable society; and a sound philosophy. They had an *unstable* society, for the nation was continually wracked either by civil war or by foreign invasions. And they held a *mystical* view of nature. Although the Hebrews scoffed at the multiplied gods of the heathen, they nonetheless gave a similar function to Yahweh. That is, they reckoned he was intimately involved in every daily event, both good and evil, natural and supernatural. For an example consider *Psalm 29*, which is simply a poetic description of an impressive thunder-storm. But no writer of our time could ever describe a storm in such terms. To the Hebrew poet God did not merely cause the storm, he *was* the storm. The thunder was his voice; the lightning was his majesty; the gale that stripped the forest bare was his fearsome hand. In terror the people flee to the temple, where they lift their voices to this awesome God. They beg him to hush the storm, to withdraw back into the heavens, and to restore peace to the land. There are many similar examples in the Old Testament. I do not mean that the Hebrews held to some kind of primitive animism, nor that they worshipped storms. But they did have a God-consciousness so intense it compelled them to connect God with even the smallest daily event. Every happening was seen as an expression of the Divine presence (cp. Is 45:7).

By contrast, the Protestant Reformers strongly denied that God was *in* a thunderstorm, or even that he was the immediate *cause* of it. Our entire society is now firmly wedded to their viewpoint. We Christians, of course, may see a reflection of the majesty and mystery of God in a splendid thunderstorm, with its stunning cacophony, and its dazzling pyrotechnics. We may respond to the heavenly display with shouts of praise, rejoicing in the matchless strength of the Almighty. But we would not call the thunder his actual voice, nor see the lightning as his manifest presence. The howling wind would not seem to us to be his invisible arm sweeping across the land. We would seldom attribute any particular storm to God's direct action.

How then do we see God? Mostly as the Author of the various natural laws that govern the changing weather patterns, which usually act independently of his direct control. No doubt the Lord God *can* intervene in the natural world whenever he chooses. But in practice we are reluctant to ascribe some natural event to a direct act of God. We tend to disown as fanatics people who go around proclaiming that some drought, flood, earthquake, or famine, was an act of divine vengeance upon sinners.[56]

---

[56] Another reason for this changed perspective, of course, is that we now have a global perspective on things. We can see (in a way that was impossible for the ancient Hebrews) that such events happen indiscriminately, and are plainly linked with environment (such as droughts in dry Australia, and floods in wet Bangladesh). We cannot help but observe that the most awful disasters often strike at

Continued on next page

A "DISENCHANTED" WORLD

The "father of modern science", Roger Bacon (13th century), gave a name to this process of rationalising the world: he called it the "disenchantment" of nature. Forests were no longer governed by wood sprites. Never again would a water demon be necessary to keep rivers flowing and tides going in and out. Caves and crannies, once dreaded as the haunt of ogres, became only pleasant places to visit. Now dawn and sunset would follow each other, and the moon wax and wane, whether or not some sacred ritual was performed.

So the "enchanted" land, mystical and incomprehensible, haunted by a thousand ghosts, became instead a mundane place, ruled only by impartial physical forces. This rejection of any fusion between God and nature, this placing of nature under the laws of God, opened the way for dispassionate study of every natural phenomenon. In a way never before possible, the world around us, stripped of its eerie nimbus, became susceptible to dissection, analysis, and utilisation.

Yet still today, a large part of the human family sees nature through ominous eyes. In thousands of villages, people still believe fervently in such things as enchanted forests, goblins, ogres, and fairies.

Suppose you were one of them; suppose you believed that a forest is bewitched, and every tree the dwelling of a magic sprite. What then? You would certainly fear to harm it. If you had to cut down a tree you would first beg forgiveness from the gods and plead for their favour. Or if you had to

Continued

---

the most helpless people - such as the thousands who are dying of hunger in North Africa as I write these words - while the more guilty enjoy apparently boundless affluence. Our concept of God usually forbids us to attribute such things to divine action (cp. Lu 9:54-55); we prefer to think of them as an impersonal outworking of natural law.

plough a field, you would first make propitiatory sacrifices. Any assault upon nature would oblige you to fulfil some magic ritual to ward off the anger of the violated demons.

Millions of people around the world still do such things every day. To them it is an act of sacrilege to treat nature impersonally, as if the earth is nothing more than something to be examined, probed, understood, and put to practical use.

But to the Reformers, and in every nation where their influence has spread, a forest is just a collection of trees, placed by God under the mandate of *Genesis 1:28-29*. The world is not supernatural, but natural. There are no sprites to appease, no goblins to bribe, no ogres to pacify; there is no magic that will increase a harvest, nor any spell to attract divine favour. People need only obey the laws of nature, and the results will be assured.

You of course take all that for granted. It would never occur to you to question it. But if the Reformation had not rid European society of its superstitions we would all still be haunted by the dreads that chained our ancestors in darkness.[57]

At once we realise that those who deny the biblical revelation are denying the very foundation upon which the achievements of our modern society have been built. Which means that Christians have a more sensible reason than atheists do for belief in that first premise of modern science:

---

[57] One notable aspect of our present society is that widespread abandonment of the Christian faith is leading inevitably to a troubling increase in superstition, seen in the use of horoscopes, astrological charts, and in the upsurge of various pagan cults. Without the witness of scripture there is no reason to believe in a rational God or an ordered world, while there are many reasons to go back to ancient mysticism. People then start looking for spells to ward off evil spirits, and for charms to attract good spirits.

nature is uniform in all its parts. For us, this belief is rational; for them it can be only a blind assumption. We base our belief upon the revelation God has given of himself in scripture. For their belief, they have no ground at all.

Even thoughtful atheists have been obliged to admit this. In an address given at Columbia University in 1950, the eminent British philosopher and mathematician Bertrand Russell, who rejected the Christian faith, said to "a stunned audience"-

> "If you have Christian love, you have a motive for existence, a guide for action, a reason for courage, *an imperative necessity for intellectual honesty.*"[58]

But Augustine realised the same thing long ago -

> "Either led astray by their own speculations or deluded by demons (pagan) thinkers reached the belief that there are many gods who must be won over to serve human ends, and also that they have, as it were, different departments with different responsi-bilities attached. Thus the body is the department of one god, the mind that of another; and within the body itself, one god is in charge of the head, another of the neck, and so on with each of the separate members. ...

> "(In) the accessories of life there are separate gods over the departments of flocks, grain, wine, oil,

---

[58] Quoted in an article, Science: From the Womb of Religion, by physicist Dr Stanley L. Jaki, in "Christian Century" October 7, 1987; pg. 851. In the same article the author mentions that when Einstein was asked why science was such a new phenomenon in human history, he dismissed the question by calling it "unfathomable". Dr Jaski then says: "Yet the question why science did not arise in any of the great ancient cultures is one of the most important questions that can be raised about human history."

forests, coinage, navigation, war and victory, marriage, birth, fertility, and so on. The Heavenly City, in contrast, knows only one God as the object of worship, and decrees, with faithful devotion, that he only is to be served ...

"(As for) the view that everything is uncertain, the City of God roundly condemns such doubt as being madness. In matters apprehended by the mind and the reason it has most certain knowledge ... (for it) believes also in the holy Scriptures, the old and the new, which we call canonical, whence is derived the faith which is the basis of the just man's life ... "[59]

---

[59] Op. cit., Bk. 19.17 & 18; pg. 877-879.

ADDENDUM

PRIMITIVE ENGLAND

Lord Lytton's novel *The Last of the Barons* is set in 15th century England, just before the Reformation. One of its characters is Adam Warner who is struggling to build a primitive steam engine, but cannot succeed. He is hampered by his own superstitious ignorance, and also by the fears of his neighbours, who reckon him a blasphemous wizard, in league with Satan.

In one scene (Book One, Chapter Eight), a young nobleman (Marmaduke Nevile) visits the aged scholar and sees a demonstration of the machine -

> Adam dragged the wondering Marmaduke to his model, or Eureka, as he had fondly named the contrivance. Marmaduke then perceived that it was from the interior of this machine that the sound which had startled him arose; to his eye the THING was uncouth and hideous; from the jaws of an iron serpent, that, wreathing round it, rose on high with erect crest, gushed a rapid volume of black smoke, and a damp spray fell around. A column of iron in the centre kept in perpetual and regular motion, rising and sinking successively, as the whole mechanism within seemed alive with noise and action.
>
> "The Syracusan[60] asked an inch of earth, beyond the earth, to move the earth," said Adam; "I stand *in* the

---

[60] Archimedes (circa B.C. 200), who said, "Give me a place to stand, and a lever long enough, and I will move the earth."

world, and lo! with this engine the world shall one day be moved."

"Holy Mother!" faltered Marmaduke; "I pray thee, dread sir, to ponder well ere thou attemptest any such sports with the habitation in which every woman's son is so concerned. ... " (he began to retreat with great trepidation and haste to the door) ... "Pardon me, terrible sir, but I have heard that the fiends are mighty malignant to all lookers-on, not initiated."

"While he spoke, fast gushed the smoke, heavily heaved the fairy hammers, up and down, down and up, sank or rose the column, with its sullen sound. The young man's heart sank to the soles of his feet ... and he fairly rushed through the open door, and hurried out of the chamber as fast as possible. He breathed more freely as he descended the stair. "Before I would call that gray carle my father, or his child my wife, may I feel all the hammers of the elves and sprites he keeps tortured within that ugly little prison-house playing a death's march on my body!"

So the young lord hastened away, trying to ward off with sundry prayers the ill effects of the wizard's demon-haunted machine. Likewise, Lytton tells how the scholar's experiments instilled terror among his neighbours who were not loathe to pelt the old man with stones, and tried to burn down his house.

But then neither was Adam Warner himself free from superstitious ignorance -

It was the misfortune to science in those days, not only that all books and mathematical instruments were enormously dear, but that the students, still struggling into light, through the glorious delusions of alchemy and mysticism - imagined that, even in simple practical operations, there were peculiar virtues in virgin gold and certain precious stones. (So he concluded that for it to work) the axle of a certain wheel must be composed of a diamond. ... Nor was this all - the diamond was to be no vulgar diamond: it was to be endowed, by talismanic skill, with certain properties and virtues; it was to be for a certain number of hours exposed to the rays of the full moon; it was to be washed in a primitive and wondrous elixir, the making of which consumed no little of the finest gold. This diamond was to be to the machine what the soul is to the body - a glorious, all-pervading, mysterious principle and activity and life.

Lytton has scattered several other illustrations of the sort through his meticulously researched novel. Not until the reasonable doctrines of Christ, as taught by the Reformers, had taken firm root in Europe were such idle fancies finally banished from the minds of scholars and researchers. Science as we know it was then born.

58

Chapter Three

MORE ASSUMPTIONS

The 19th century American philosopher and essayist Ralph Waldo Emerson, in his great work *Introduction to Nature*, wrote:

> "Undoubtedly we have no questions to ask which are unanswerable. We must trust the perfection of creation so far as to believe that whatever curiosity the order of things has awakened in our minds, the order of things can satisfy."

Undoubtedly that claim is largely true. And it leads to a second assumption that undergirds modern science -

NATURE IS UNDERSTANDABLE

Scientists approach nature, not only with the belief that it is *uniform* (as we saw in the previous chapter), but also that it is *understandable* - that is, it will yield its secrets to rational research. In scientific circles you will often find statements like the one just below, taken from an article in *Geo*[61] magazine. The article describes modern man's quest for a consistent and unified theory, one that fully explains how the physical universe works. Then it raises a question about the modern assumption that such a theory must surely be achievable -

> "(Is this) an arrogant assumption? Perhaps. But it is the same arrogance that has marked mankind's view throughout recorded history, that there is a key to

---

[61] July 1981, pg. 21.

> the way the world functions, and that this key can be uncovered by human thought."

There most surely is an "arrogance" in such statements, for (apart from scripture) there is no rational ground upon which they can stand. There is also a misunderstanding of history. It is not true to suggest that intelligent men and women have *always* thought that the human mind could create a unified theory of the universe. As we have seen, the opposite has been more generally the case. Of course, people have usually believed that there is *some* "key" to the mystery of the universe. But they have been prone to find that key, not in diligent research, but in religious superstition, and in myth and legend. Their cultural milieu has encouraged them to abandon curious thought, rather than to utilise it.

Even the atheistic scientist Sir Fred Hoyle was obliged to acknowledge this. Commenting on the greatest mystery of all, the origin of life, and the many theories that have been propounded, awash with anomalies and absurdities, he said

> "Another fuddled notion is that life began here on earth in a brew of organic material. The mystery is why grown men and women have allowed themselves to be persuaded into such beliefs, in spite of there being a considerable body of fact running against them."[62]

Never let facts get in the way of a good theory! Yet we do feel that the quest for a unified theory is correct; Emerson's proposition after all does seem reasonable. Let us but ask the right questions in the right way, and surely nature will eventually yield her secrets and her benefits. But we are entitled to ask: what sufficient cause can anyone have for such a belief? Nature itself offers no such guarantee. On the

---

[62] Quoted by Casti, op. cit. pg. 120.

contrary, every society on earth that has lacked biblical influence, has viewed nature supernaturally, not naturally.

When the European settlers first arrived in North America they grossly offended the indigenous peoples (mistakenly called Red Indians) by their assault upon the earth. They ravaged the fields with their ploughs; they slew the forests with their saws and axes. The natives saw those actions as raping their Mother, or blaspheming their god.

Similarly, in Australia a quarrel continues between European and Aboriginal culture. The utilitarian western view of the earth and of its minerals clashes against the deeply mystical and religious view of the Aborigines. The spiritual "bonding" with the land affirmed by indigenous people is incomprehensible to most white Australians. It sounds to them like a silly superstition, and they find it difficult to treat the Aboriginal view patiently and tolerantly.

Yet western culture embraces only a minority of Earth's inhabitants. Around the world today, as in the past, millions of people remain chained to magic rituals. They cannot take a plough or a sickle into a field without first making a sacrifice, offering a prayer, or casting a spell. They would not dare to carry an axe into a forest without first performing the necessary sacred rituals. They have a superstitious dread of pressing any enquiry into the nature of things too far.

That should not seem too strange to us, because echoes of such things from our own not-so-distant-past can still be found in popular sayings: "There are things we just aren't meant to know;" or, "Finally they've gone too far!" - and the like.

Augustine tells how, among the Romans, when a woman had given birth to a child, she had to follow a particular ritual. Its purpose was to protect her from Sylvanus, a wild and savage forest god, who lusted horribly after the new mother. Her protection was found in three domestic deities, upon whom she had to call to guard her and her infant from attack by Sylvanus. The presence of those custodian deities was symbolised by three men, whose task it was, for a certain number of nights, to visit each door of the house. One carried an axe, the other a pestle, and the third a large broom. They had to strike each threshold with the axe and the pestle, and then sweep it with the broom. The use of these agricultural tools against the untamed forest demon was thought sufficient to drive him away, and so protect the lady of the house until her strength was fully recovered.[63]

People who believe such stuff (and there are still millions who do) cannot approach research with the dispassionate objectivity required of a scientist. Our own escape from such stifling fallacies stems from the new way the Reformers looked at scripture. They saw in the inspired page a picture of a wholly natural world subject to the unchanging will of one Almighty God. Once that idea had taken root, the way was open for investigation and discovery to begin. The earth, the rocks, the forests, the lakes, the rivers, the fields, could be approached without dread, analysed without fear, employed without taboos.

The Reformers never doubted that God was willing to help researchers to unfold all the marvels of nature, and so gain use of all the riches of the planet. But if Reformation doctrine is denied, what basis remains for that confidence? Yet even agnostic scientists proceed on the assumption that nature is and will remain understandable. For them, far more than for us, it is an act of unsupported and unsupportable faith.

---

[63]   Op. cit. Bk. VI.9.

A RELIABLE MIND

ARE YOU A DELUSION?

Is your mind reliable? Can its processes be trusted? That problem has bothered many philosophers, but there seems to be no final answer. We act every day on the presumption that we can trust the evidence of our senses, taking it for granted that we can rely upon the way our mind thinks. Yet how easily the mind can be deceived! You have no doubt been the embarrassed victim of an optical illusion, or of some magic trick, where appearances proved sadly deceptive. Or you may have visited a technology or science museum, where displays were set up for the express purpose of causing people to see what is not there. At any rate, you know that your eyes and ears are not *always* reliable; they can convey a false message. Your senses can persuade you to see what is not there, or not to see what is there! They can make you accept as true what is actually a lie.

Recognising this, some philosophers have wondered if we can *ever* trust our perceptions? I have read at least one report of students being driven to suicide when a clever professor cast dark doubt upon their true identity: *"How do you know you are what you think you are?"* Or consider a man in an asylum who thinks he is Napoleon. You cannot *prove* to him that *his* perception is wrong while yours is correct. He trusts the evidence of *his* mind as much as you trust *yours*. Yet what better ground for that trust do you have than he has? How do you know that some unseen sorcerer is not deceiving you every moment of the day? Perhaps everything that is happening around you is the product of a magic spell? Cannot a hypnotist trick people into supposing that they are cats, or dogs, or frogs? Perhaps we are all of us, all the time, suffering from a similar mass delusion? Perhaps after all "life is but a dream"!

A school of philosophy called "solipsism" has developed around this enigma. It holds that the human mind has no ground for believing in anything but itself. Presumably the mind is truly there, because it is raising questions about its own existence. But beyond that it cannot "prove" that anything else exists except its inner perceptions. After all, the impressions we have of light, darkness, sound, people, and an array of other things, are in the end nothing more than images in the receptors of our minds. If the mind did not register those images we would never know that anything existed.

This was the starting point of the philosophy of the great Frenchman, Descartes (1596-1650). Assuming that the mind could not doubt unless it were actually there to express that doubt, he coined the famous affirmation: *Cogito, ergo sum!* - "I think, therefore I am!" Descartes went on from that point to "prove" the existence of the larger world also. But his arguments are not finally convincing. So the true solipsist remains convinced that the only reality a person can truly affirm is his own existence. For all I know, the rest of the world is an illusion!

Some schools of Buddhism enshrine that very idea. They insist that nothing truly exists except the self. Everything else is a false perception. Even the self is only semi-real. It is like a piece of floating spray, whose ultimate destiny is to fall back into the vast sea whence it was flung. Merged again with the great ocean, each fleck of wind-tossed foam loses its independent existence and identity. Likewise the soul, wrongfully separated from the divine being, must one day fall back into Brahma, and be no more.

Similar ideas have been expressed in various ways by many philosophers, both oriental and western. In practice we trust the processes of our minds, and rely upon our perceptions. Yet there seems to be no real basis for that trust, and many reasons to question it.

WHO THEN IS SANE?

So we are back to our question: how do the sane know that their perception of reality is more trustworthy than that of the insane? In the end the only "proof" that exists is statistics: there are more of us than there are of them!

Suppose every person in the world were blind except you. A day comes when you try to tell the others about light and colour, to describe a rose, to portray a rainbow, to paint verbally a sunset! Who do you think would be branded a lunatic and locked up?

So then, what is rational depends to a great degree upon how many people there are who agree on the matter. If you stand with the majority you will be reckoned sane; if you stand with the minority you will be reckoned insane!

Yet we cannot allow such arguments. We remain quite certain that the lunatic is wrong and that we are right. The world we see is real, but his is false. And this confidence is not based on mere statistics, but rather on an innate awareness - that is, upon *faith*!

Indeed, that faith is needed more now than ever before, for science is showing that our perceptions *cannot* altogether be trusted. No two people ever see exactly the same thing. Think about how differently the four gospel writers saw Jesus! On a less exalted level, consider the different perceptions of those whom the majority rather arrogantly call "colour-blind". Again it is a matter of statistics; because there are more of us than of them, we call our sight "normal" and theirs "abnormal". But suppose the numbers were reversed? Who then would be deemed as having "normal" sight? But even among those whose sight is reckoned "normal" it is still true that we see and feel things differently. Again, some people can so condition themselves mentally that they become immune to pain. They stab themselves with skewers, scorch themselves with flame, feel no pain, and not even a mark remains on their skin!

So then what *is* reality? Is the *real* world the one you see? Or the one I see?

Or think about Jesus again. After his resurrection he had flesh and bones, yet could appear and disappear at will, pass through solid walls, and traverse the gulf between heaven and earth. Which world then is real; mine or his? In *my* world, a corporeal body cannot drift through a brick wall; but in *his* world, it can!

I plan to return to this mystery of perception later.[64] For now though, the point is that apart from instinct and statistics, people who reject the biblical revelation have no valid basis upon which to trust the processes of the human mind. Yet every scientist trusts those processes absolutely, for all intelligent research is based upon that very premise. It remains a "given" of the entire scientific enterprise that the human mind is a reliable tool. But it cannot be "proved". We Christians alone have any truly rational grounds upon which to trust our minds. We do so because scripture says that we are made in the image of a rational God, who himself invites us to "reason together" with him.

INDUCTION AS A METHOD

Before we leave this part of our discussion, note one more thing. Modern science is primarily based upon *induction* (that is arguing from the particular to the general). But no amount of supporting evidence is ever enough to confirm any inductive hypothesis beyond all doubt, for it takes only one piece of contradictory evidence to refute it. This is well illustrated by the familiar footprint in the sand analogy.

---

[64] See under Section (V) below; and the next Chapter, plus the Addendum that follows it.

Suppose you amass a great quantity of data to prove that no-one has ever walked along a particular beach. Is your argument secure? No, for unless you have physically inspected that beach every day since the moment it was created, your hypothesis must remain unproved. Yet just one footprint will destroy it absolutely! In other words, it takes an incredible amount of evidence to prove that something has *never* happened; but only *one* item to prove that it has![65]

THE SIMPLER THE BETTER

One of the great principles that undergirds the modern scientific endeavour is known as *"Ockham's Razor"*. This was a philosophical notion developed by William of Ockham in the early 14th century. It is known also as *The Principle of Parsimony*, and its usual formulation is: *Entities must not be multiplied beyond necessity"* - that is, the preferred explanation of any phenomenon is the one that is simplest and least cluttered. Hence the name "razor" - from the idea of "shaving" an argument to its simplest terms by cutting away from it all unnecessary complications.

For example, gravity could be explained as a force-field flung around the earth by an alien, to prevent any human from ever escaping this solar system. Against such fancies, Sir Isaac Newton in the late 17th century used Ockham's rule and propounded his beautifully simple "law": *every mass exerts an attraction upon every other mass*, and at once all of Newtonian physics became possible. Indeed, Newton conceived his own form of the "Razor": admit nothing into a definition beyond what is necessary to explain a phenomenon. To that he added another rule: use the same

---

[65] I will come back to this idea in Part Two, when we consider the evidence for God's existence.

cause to explain as many effects as possible; that is, do not needlessly multiply causes.

William of Ockham applied his theory mainly to philosophy and theology, and by it derided the fantastic superstitions that in his time were promulgated even by the church. He insisted that the simplest theory necessary to explain the known facts of religion is the one that should always be adopted. But the beauty of his rule was widely recognised, and just as widely applied. It became one of the fundamental axioms of scientific research. Without "Ockham's Razor" modern science could hardly have developed, for it opened up ways of viewing the world that were previously nearly impossible. Think, for example, about the mythical and fantastic explanations the ancients had of various phenomena: the god Thor, striking his anvil with a great hammer and causing thunder; the various myths of the Greeks about the causes of the changing seasons, snow, falling rain, lightning, the darkening skies of evening; the similar myths of the Egyptians, the Romans; etc.

We should be grateful that for us such amusing fancies belong only in children's story books. Yet acceptance of "Ockham's Razor" is not based upon any kind of rational proof, but rather upon an intuitive sense of its rightness. It is a scholar's dogma, not an objective fact; it is an article of *faith*, a principle that is "known" to be true, yet one that cannot be "proved".

"Ockham's Razor" is appealing to Christians. We may well argue that no one will ever formulate a simpler or more satisfying explanation of the origin of things than the one given in the Bible: *"In the beginning, God created the heavens and the earth"* (Ge 1:1).

CAUSE AND EFFECT

When I was in high school (nearly five decades ago) I was taught that at least one scientific "law" was immutable and totally dependable: the law of "cause and effect" - that is, for every effect there had to be a sufficient cause; action and reaction are equal and opposite. However, it is now recognised that this "law" cannot be "proved" to be anything more than a statistical assessment. That is, based upon past happenings, we can calculate the presumed probability that an event will continue to happen. The greater the number of individual happenings, the more likely it is that a pattern will emerge; but the emerging pattern is never absolutely certain, for any one of a million chances may alter it forever.

NOT SO OBVIOUS

In this matter, the ancients were once again possibly more rational than modern man. They did *not* believe that cause and effect would always and surely follow each other. They lived in dread that tomorrow might not be the same as today. Each morning superstitious societies around the world have offered sacrifices to guarantee the rising of the sun. They were far from certain that the dawn would arrive automatically, as it always has. Similar sacrifices, incantations, and the like, were offered in connection with harvest time, the growth of forests, the change of seasons, and so on.

In ancient Egypt (as in other societies that have depended upon the flow of a river) elaborate rituals and sacrifices were presented to the gods at different times of the year to ensure the rise of the Nile.

The deeply religious, and highly superstitious, Romans, as we have seen, found it necessary to secure divine help for everything in life. Unless a god acted, nothing could happen; and even then it would happen *correctly* (that is, to human benefit) only if the relevant deity had been well humoured. [66] Hence a significant part of each day was devoted by sincere

---

[66] See the City of God Bk IV.21; 19.17.

Romans to intoning the various prayers, incantations, spells, benedictions, graces, and the like, that were necessary to persuade each deity to behave kindly.[67]

WHY ARE WE WISE?

Why have *we* abandoned that way of relating to the world? How is that *we* know (as Henri Bergson wrote) that *"the present contains nothing more than the past"*. Why is it that for us it is axiomatic that *"cause and effect"* is a rule that truly can be relied upon. Why are we so wise when our fathers were not? Simply because the time finally came when the revolutionary idea expressed in the Bible was finally understood: *"I am the Lord, I never change!"* (Ma 3:6). Or, as William Cowper expressed it, *"nature is but an effect, whose cause is God"*

After Nature was stripped of capricious willfulness, it became at once subject to divine law. Now scholars could approach a phenomenon with the attitude that a natural and explicable cause underlay it. Modern science became possible. Yet apart from the biblical revelation, and the way it has shaped our consciousness, this "law" of cause and effect would have remained unrealised. Indeed, it still sits uncomfortably with many people. Mark the continuing immense popularity of fantasy stories, and the still widespread belief in ghosts and other preternatural marvels.

The strength of the ancient delusion can be seen even in the church. There are still Christians who mix with their faith a mystical approach to life that is barely one step away from the old superstitions. They are constantly surprised when the unfeeling rule of "cause and effect" works upon them

---

[67] This ancient theory still might have provided a rational base for scientific thought if all the gods had acted in unity; but when they were seen as constantly warring against each other, and against humanity, who could be sure of anything?

remorselessly. They cannot understand why no good angel comes to rescue them from the inevitable results of foolish choices or actions!

Why do people keep on venturing into such folly? Simply because they are unwilling to accept the rule that effect must always follow cause. They prefer to believe that the consequences of their actions are *not* inevitable. And in a sense, who can blame them? For it is no more obvious today than it was in the past - from mere observation of the world - that cause and effect *must* irresistibly follow each other. Skepticism about this matter is more rational than belief. Yet sensible people remain convinced, whether or not the link can be proved logically, that the "law" of cause and effect must be trusted. Science too continues to act upon a firm presumption of its truth. But if it cannot be proved, then it is still...

AN ARTICLE OF FAITH

"(Many scientists find) a kind of natural religion in science that gives them their answer to some of the cosmic questions. And the principle element of that religion - or 'faith' - is a belief that everything that happens in the world has a scientific explanation, for every effect there is a cause. It is not a supernatural cause, but one that physics can explain and understand. *There is no proof of that ...* And that's why I call this *an article of faith* among my colleagues"[68]

Or consider the following "leap of faith" that scientists must make -

---

[68] Science laureate and agnostic, Robert Jastrow, in an article "A Scientist Caught Between Two Faiths", Christianity Today, Aug 6, 1982. Emphasis mine.

> "Einstein showed that matter is a form of energy, and that particles cannot be thought of as separate from the space that surrounds them ... Quantum theory, in fact, characterises particles as having only 'a tendency to exist'; we can deduce their existence and natures from the cloud trails they leave in bubble chambers or the impressions they make upon photographic materials. Thus modern science is confronted with the kinds of mysteries theologians have been intimate with for centuries; *merely stating that particles exist requires a leap of faith.*"[69]

And here is another statement, by a scientist, expressing the growing mystery that is penetrating modern research -

> "That particles can act like waves may seem bizarre.[70] But no more so than some other oddities suggested by quantum theory: that how we probe matter affects its behaviour and form; that some particles exist so briefly that they are not real but 'virtual'; and that well-ordered reality - the whole of the universe - rests on chance and randomness at the sub-atomic level. ... Atoms are 'messy' to our conventional way of thinking about objects. As described by the Heisenberg uncertainty principle and the whole of quantum theory, the kind of objects they seem to be depends on how we observe them. But by our observation we alter their states. ...

---

[69] From an article, "Visions Of A New Faith", in Science Digest, Nov 1981.

[70] The reference is to sub-atomic particle research, where the most amazing, and sometimes weird phenomena are observed. As the author says, physicists hardly know what to make of their own discoveries. See also the next Chapter, and the Addendum that follows it.

Observation not only affects reality but in a way creates it - we can choose to measure light as particles or waves ... The strangeness of quantum reality has led some thinkers to speculate that reality is a meaningless idea and others to ponder mysticism."[71]

A WEIRD WORLD

So scientists are saying that matter, energy, and space are interchangeable, and there is no way of predicting which will occur (a superficial analogy can be seen in vapour, water, and ice: each is potentially becoming the other). Underlying the visible world is a sub-atomic world of astonishing randomness, where almost nothing is predictable.

Quantum mechanics, for example, offers undeniable proof that electrons are *waves*; but it also offers undeniable proof that they are tiny *particles*. So what are they? In photographs of particle or electron trails we see little dots of light, like tiny billiard balls. Except that whether or not those balls are really there, whether they are moving or stationary, are matters for the observer to choose! If he says they are simply bursts of energy, so they are. If he says they truly exist, so they do. If he says they are moving, behold they move. If he says they are fixed in place, behold they are. His observing of them, the choices he makes about them, all affect reality.

Suppose you design an experiment to measure wave properties, then the electron obediently behaves like a *wave*. Design an experiment to measure matter properties: it just as obediently behaves like a *particle*. Design an experiment to measure *both* properties, and the electron will cheerfully display both properties. It seems to behave in response to whatever the experimenter wishes. Impossibly, the electron

---

[71] From an article "Worlds Within the Atom" by John Boslough; "National Geographic" magazine, May 1985, pg. 641,642,649.

seems to be aware, not just of its own narrow path, but of the entire environment in which the experiment is being conducted, including the presence of the observer.

That description is perhaps badly over-simplified; but it shows clearly enough the weirdness represented by quantum mechanics. Everything we call "real" around us seems to be composed of things that are "unreal", almost as though they come into existence only when someone observes them! Yet we *know* that is nonsense. A tree is surely *there*, whether or not I am looking at it! But those are the conundrums that physicists are stirring up in their laboratories.

Even Albert Einstein, who helped to develop quantum theories, was unable to find a way to resolve the bewildering paradoxes that exist at the sub-atomic level. It truly does seem crazy to say that merely observing something changes its nature and behaviour. It makes you dizzy just thinking about it! We begin to feel like the drunk who was returning to his Parisian garret after spending an evening in a tavern with a friend. As he staggered down the road, he imagined he was making the whole universe spin -

> Think how queer it is!
> Every move I'm making,
> Cosmic gravity's
> Centre I am shaking;
>
> Oh, how droll to feel
> (As I now am feeling)
> Even as I reel,
> All the world is reeling!
>
> Reeling too the stars,
> Neptune and Uranus,
> Jupiter and Mars,
> Mercury and Venus;
>
> Suns and moons with me,
> As I'm homeward straying,

> All in sympathy
> Swaying, swaying, swaying.[72]

The astonishing thing is that quantum mechanics has shown that in some sense your presence on the earth, and mine, does somehow affect the very universe! Queer though it sounds, even the most distant galaxy seems to "know" we are here, and is changed by it. The whimsical poet said a lot more than he supposed!

A BUTTERFLY IN BRAZIL

The recent development of "Chaos Theory" has demonstrated the same truth in a different way by showing the uncanny inter-relatedness of everything. One popular statement of it says that a butterfly may flutter in Brazil and the result will be a tornado in Japan! Yet thoughtful people have always been aware of this unsettling principle -

> "Wondrous truly are the bonds that unite us one and all; whether by the soft binding of Love, or the iron chaining of necessity... I say, there is not a Red Indian, hunting by Lake Winnipic, can quarrel with his squaw, but the whole world must smart for it: will not the price of beaver rise? It is a mathematical fact that the casting of this pebble from my hand alters the centre of gravity of the Universe!"[73]

But if randomness is at the heart of the universe, how does one explain the seemingly fixed patterns we see everywhere? Answer: those patterns arise out of the sheer number of particles from which the whole is made. Suppose you begin

---

[72] Robert Service. From Ballads of a Bohemian: "Spring"; stanzas 7 & 8 of "Noctambule" (April 1914); T. Fisher Unwin, London, 1921; pg. 32.

[73] Thomas Carlyle, op. cit. Book Three, Chapter Seven. Note that he wrote those words 150 years ago, long before Quantum or Chaos theories were even thought of!

to drop some coloured balls onto the ground. If you have only a few balls, they will seem to fall in a haphazard pattern - one here, one there, scattering randomly. You cannot tell where they will come to rest. But if you drop huge numbers of balls, patterns will begin to emerge that are all but 100% predictable. The same is true of people. One person's behaviour may be uncertain; no insurance company can say with certainty whether his life will be short or long. But the actions of a million people are so thoroughly predictable that reliable actuarial tables are based upon them.

Thus one particle may behave randomly; but when there are trillions of them patterns emerge that turn into the solid world we touch every day. Yet those forms remain only statistical averages, and are therefore not wholly certain. Randomness remains the last word, from a purely scientific point of view, about the universe. Here is a paradox indeed! Science depends for its enterprise upon acceptance of certain axioms, without which its work cannot proceed; yet that very work, instead of proving the truth of the axioms, appears to be undermining them! Where then shall we turn for certainty? Shall we abandon the assumptions upon which rational thought is based?

No, for at the practical level of daily life - even of scientific life - our assumptions remain as validly and instinctively true as ever. But it does mean that we find ourselves confronted with mystery beyond anything the ancients imagined. We are faced also with a demand for humility in the presence of things that no test tube can ever contain. The need for a "leap of faith" becomes stronger than ever before!

A DEEP ENIGMA

We also discover that science cannot rely upon so-called objective fact alone (even if there is such a thing). In other words, there is a deep enigma at the heart of science, just as there is at the heart of religion (1 Co 13:12). Some things no scientist will ever "prove", they can only be believed -

"I think the man of science must be willing to admit that he does not have the ultimate grip upon reality - that what he calls reality or scientific truth is ephemeral. As the scientific view of the world is completely different from that of 300 years ago, so there are other views that will replace his. He must keep an open mind to those who may have some perception of the larger meaning and of truths that are not within the present body of scientific knowledge.

"But scientists, and physicists especially, tend to feel that they know everything. The physicist is so successful in his narrow range of problems that he feels his techniques of thought can potentially tell him everything. It is the success of their approach to life that gives them this (closed-minded certainty)."[74]

But now that once-tidy world of the scientist, physicist, and astronomer is being rapidly demolished. Those who once thought that everything came into existence simply as an accident, a hiccup of nature, and that diligent research would remove every mystery are facing disappointment. The more the scientist reduces things to their components and tries to discover and measure the basic laws by which they operate, the more he finds himself facing paradox and perplexity. He moves from the world of physics into metaphysics - which we Christians would call by another name: the spiritual dimension.

THE ANSWER IS IN SCRIPTURE

So while the scientist finds himself plunging further into quandary, Christians open the Bible and find there report of the Creator. There we discover the Divine purpose behind the whole universe. Some great scientists, perhaps

---

[74] Robert Jastrow, op. cit.

reluctantly, are coming to recognise this. In his book *God and the Astronomers*, Robert Jastrow acknowledged that science had no solution to the problem of the ultimate cause of all things. He also wrote -

> "For the scientist who has lived by his faith in the power of reason, the story ends like a bad dream. He has scaled the mountains of ignorance; he is about to conquer the highest peak; as he pulls himself over the final rock, he is greeted by a band of theologians who have been sitting there for centuries."[75]

The theologians will still be there, waiting expectantly, when God finally brings it all to an end, and begins again with the new heavens and the new earth!

---

[75] Quoted in "Christianity Today", August 6, 1982; pg. 14. As mentioned in an earlier Footnote, Dr Jastrow (at the time of writing) was a self-avowed agnostic, sympathetic toward the Christian faith, feeling unable to accept it, but equally unable to offer an alternative.

Chapter Four

A SENSE OF WONDER

> Methinks these new Actaeons[76] boast too soon
> That they have spied on beauty; what if we
> Have analysed the rainbow, robbed the moon
> Of her most ancient, chastest mystery,
> Shall I, the last Endymion[77], lose all hope
> Because rude eyes peer at my mistress
> through a telescope?
>
> What profit if this scientific age
> Burst through our gates with all its retinue
> Of modern miracles! Can it assuage
> One lover's breaking heart? What can it do
> To make one life more beautiful, one day
> More godlike in its period?[78]

Science, which had high hopes only a few decades ago of breaking through every barrier of ignorance and of finding a single unifying explanation that would encompass all reality,

---

[76] Actaeon was a mythical Greek hunter who was turned into a stag by the goddess Artemis because he gazed upon her while she was bathing naked. Because he boasted about what he had seen, he was punished by being torn to pieces by his own former hounds. The poet sees scientists in the same guise: insisting, like Actaeon, that they have penetrated the secrets of nature, and have seen her "unclothed".

[77] In Greek mythology, Endymion was a remarkably beautiful young man who was loved by the Moon goddess. The poet views himself as the last of the Moon's true lovers, who sees her still clothed in mythical beauty, unsullied by the crass touch of unromantic science.

[78] Oscar Wilde, Garden of Eros, stanzas 38, 39.

now finds itself increasingly disappointed. Instead of demolishing boundaries, the scientist finds himself increasingly facing new and impassable walls, and an ever-growing mystery. One immense disappointment to some scientists has been the growing confirmation of the "Big Bang" theory, which argues that the entire universe began as a small piece of compressed matter. Then, eons ago, enormous pressures built up in the tiny ball and led to a stupendous explosion (the "Big Bang"). The present cosmos is the still-expanding debris of that cataclysm. If it is true, the theory means that whatever existed before the cataclysm, supposing there *was* anything, has been utterly destroyed. Therefore scientific enquiry cannot go further back than that event. A dead end has been reached. What lies on the other side of it? Science will never know.

Furthermore, the theory shows that the universe came into existence by the exertion of forces and laws that are unknown in the present world, and would not even be valid in our environment. Therefore they too must lie forever beyond human discovery. All of which is deeply dismaying to some secular scientists. Their hope is gone. Their dream of hustling God out of the cosmos by explaining everything in terms of physics and mathematics has faded away. He who sits in the heavens laughs! (Ps 2:4)

QUESTIONS WITHOUT ANSWERS

Still more dismaying to some is another realisation: science cannot explain the presence of the very things that make science itself possible. What are they? Answer: the origin of matter; the cause of life; human self-consciousness; our capacity for language;[79] the ability for logical argument; our power of deliberate rational choice; our sense of good and

---

[79] I will take up the question of the miraculous phenomenon of language in Part Two.

evil; the wondrous coherence of the universe; and many other precious qualities. The solution to those puzzles will never be squeezed out of a test tube. Christians, however, can still quote the beautifully simple words of scripture: *"In the beginning God created the heavens and the earth ... and made men and women in his own image."*

At the other end of the scale, moving from the macrocosm to the microcosm, an opposite problem has arisen. There the scientists *were* hoping to find an end to their search for the ultimate building block of the universe. When I was at school, that building block was said to be the atom. I can still remember sitting in physics class and droning out the definition, "An atom is the smallest indivisible piece of matter." Then came the mushroom cloud, and the text books had to be re-written. The atom was split, and then split again, and again, and again, until now the particles have become unimaginably infinitesimal. Electrons are so insubstantial that it becomes a matter of choice whether they are called matter or mere pulses of energy. Yet it seems there will never be any end to the number of times they can be "split".

The more deeply physicists penetrate into the nuclear world, the more they find themselves plunging into a realm of apparently random chaos and pure swirling force. Yet out of this anarchy has arisen a universe of amazing structural coherence and ordered beauty! Reason finds itself transcended by awe.

Some Christians have been unduly troubled by this underlying chaos. But the inherent randomness of the universe, far from suggesting that the development of life is a pure accident, shows the opposite. Contrary to Bertrand Russell, who declared that even human life is merely the result of "accidental collocations of atoms", we say the evidence points in several ways to design and purpose -

(1) Surely the bringing of order out of chaos is indicative of a controlling hand guided by a rational purpose? At least that would be our automatic conclusion in any other sphere of life. Admittedly, the rules that apply in the sub-atomic realm are often remote from those that control the larger world, but the same ultimate logic applies. If that were not so, then intelligent people would not be able to formulate theories about atoms, nor offer any rational explanation of their behaviour.

(2) The tiny pieces out of which all things are built do have an inbuilt coherence, a definite potentiality, an inner "drive" toward organising themselves (or being organised) into larger bodies. They seem to have an ultimate compulsion toward the formation of life itself. Were that not so, then no atoms would ever collect into molecules, or molecules into still larger forms. So it is not true to say that chaos is the dominant factor in the universe. Certainly, the foundations seem to be laid among sub-atomic randomness; but there remains an over-riding pressure toward coherence.[80]

(3) It has been said that the existence of chaos at the particle level argues against there being any design or purpose in the universe. But why must that be so? The very chaos itself can be seen as part of God's design, for it allows the utmost possible variety of shape. Out of this randomness, new kinds of matter and new forms of life can constantly emerge; it is the best way of trying out all possible

---

[80] I am aware of the rule of entropy - the proposition that all things have an inbuilt tendency toward decay and collapse; they tend to fall into disorder, and ultimately back into chaos. There is plainly a tension between the working of entropy in the world and the renewing force of life. Both forces are at work in the world. Christian theology blames sin as the cause of entropy. Yet still there seems to be an inbuilt impulse among the chaos of the sub-nuclear level toward integration and life.

combinations. The marvelous diversity of mineral, plant, and animal forms that fill the earth so profusely show what a kaleidoscope of arrangement may arise out of random freedom! So the capacity of sub-nuclear forces and particles of matter to blend in an infinite number of ways is itself part of the Creator's design. We see in it one aspect of his method of Creation.

This restless flux shows also that the cosmos is not static. The processes of creation are as active and dynamic now as they have ever been. Perhaps Jesus had something like this in mind when he said, *"My Father is still working, and I am working!"* (Jn 5:17). The Father is no mere "God-of-the-gaps". He sustains a continuous, all-pervasive creative and controlling relationship with every part of the universe. This too was expressed by the apostle long ago: *"He holds all things together by the word of his power"* (He 1:3).

AN ELEGANT BALANCE

Here is another astonishing discovery: the basic constituents of the universe are joined together in an amazing inter-relationship. The bond is so intricate that even a minute change in a single equation could disrupt the whole. Nowhere is that more true than in the existence of life on Earth. The balance of forces is so exquisitely delicate that even a minute variation would snuff out all life like a candle flame in a gusty wind. An astonishing exactness is required of an infinite array of numerical constants. Alter just one formula and our planet would be wrecked, turning perhaps into a baking desert, or a frozen wilderness. Life is possible only because a vast number of variables are precisely fixed at their optimum values. Yet there is no logical reason why those equations should not be different. Trillions of changes are possible. Which means that the chances of the elegant balance that does exist occurring by accident are remote almost beyond calculation. The universe gives the appearance of being deliberately structured to support this planet and its prolific life. The question of why this is so, lies altogether beyond any scientific solution. We must look elsewhere for those kinds of answers.

THE MYSTERY OF THE MIND

One of the most baffling problems confronting modern thinkers is the way the mind interprets reality. Does the world have an existence that is independent of our perception of it. Is nature just *there*, whether or not someone observes it? Do the images that form in our minds when we look around us *exactly* mirror reality, or only *partially*, or not at all? Does what you see actually exist, or is it in fact something very different? I have raised these questions already, in a different context, and we will come back to them again in the Addendum that follows this chapter. But let us look at them here from a special angle.

Most people naturally assume that what they see is what is there. On any other assumption life would be impossible. Nor could anyone prove us wrong. Let someone try to tell me that a green tree is a brown cow and I will question, not my sanity, but his!

Nonetheless, many experiments have shown that our minds are, and must be, highly selective in what information they are willing to receive. Facing an incessant bombardment every moment of the day by millions of pieces of data, your mind automatically turns aside large quantities of that avalanche. The remainder it organises in different ways. To some data it gives great prominence, while other pieces are rated at various levels, from importance to near total obscurity. Out of these siftings the mind compiles a set of images that are meaningful to its owner.

None of that is particularly surprising. What *has* amazed modern researchers is the realisation that the mind does all this *according to an already existing template*. That is, from the moment of birth each person's mind is already predisposed to recognise certain images. Out of the torrent of information that keeps pouring into it, the mind accepts whatever fits one of those templates, and rejects (or at best files away for possible future use) the remainder.

When you think about it, the mind could not function any other way. Suppose the mind were to give the same importance to every item that reaches it. What then? The tumultuous chaos of data, the sheer overwhelming abundance of it, would soon create a massive information overload, and the mind would be crushed. Consider for example a painting. Only a foolish artist would try to give equal prominence to every detail in a picture. Such a painting would be meaningless, just a shapeless mass of many colours. Or if he tried to record on canvas every item of the scene that lies before him, the same result must follow. Rather, he must select from the scene no more than is necessary for his purpose. Even what he chooses to record with his brush must be arranged so that some items are highlighted while others fall into the background.

Note though, that the artist fills in his canvas according to a design he has already chosen. That is what happens in all of us. The mind seems to measure incoming data against standard patterns that are embedded in it from birth. Whatever agrees with those patterns is welcomed; whatever is incongruent is cast aside.

Now this destroys the still widely held idea that every baby arrives in the world with a blank mind (like a clean slate), upon which is scratched the experiences of each day. Those marks (it was once thought) gradually build up into a coherent picture of reality. The child learns by trial and error alone; no inborn grasp of the world, no innate sense of what to look for and what to reject, exists in its mind. That view is now obsolete. Without a standard to measure things by, nothing could be measured. We are born with that template, and begin to fit things into it from the moment we first open our eyes.

Parallel to this, consider the world of *abstract* art. A gifted abstract painter reverses the normal visual process. He goes, as it were, back to an earlier mental stage. He compels his mind to stop before it begins to sort out the confusion of inrushing data; he tries to see what is there before the mind has arranged it into recognisable shapes. His maelstrom of colours, his formless images, show how we might all see the world if our minds did not instinctively arrange the turbulent flood of incoming information into pre-determined images.

Clearly then, no one could build a useful picture of the world from experience alone. Without a set of already existing, innate, concepts we would have no criteria upon which to sort out the data or attach any meaning to it. That, of course, remains true throughout life. No one, young or old, can interpret any event (that is, give useful meaning to it) without some pre-existing criteria by which to assess it . We keep on adding to those criteria across the years, but we all began with a basic inborn set. The question is, where did those templates come from? Some say they are transmitted genetically, a product of evolution. Others reply that the cause is inadequate for the result. The Christian sees them as implanted by God.[81]

THE MYSTERY OF CONGRUENCE

But there is a still greater mystery. How does it happen that the innate rules by which we interpret our experiences fit so well the world in which we live? An almost endless variety of internal "templates" are imaginable. How did we come to get just the right set? How do they stay so constant throughout the entire human family? What are the chances of this

---

[81] See the last item in the Addendum at the end of this chapter for an experiment in vision.

amazing fit occurring by mere accident? Once again, some are content with a mechanistic or evolutionary explanation; but others believe the mystery is too great, the opposing odds too staggering, to admit such a superficial solution.

Think about a computer. Despite its marvelous complexity it remains useless until it is equipped with a software program that enables it to process data. That software must also fit two other things: the kind of data the operator will put into the computer; and the output required from it. One piece of software will enable the computer to handle a mass of *numbers*; another will allow it to work with *words*; another with graphic *images*; and so on. The computer can make sense of informational input, and produce a useful result, only when that information is channeled through a pre-installed and appropriate software package. In just the same way our minds seem to have been programmed in the womb to process data, and then produce a pre-determined result. It is this that turns the brain into a *mind*, just as software turns a piece of machinery into a *computer*.

Yet we are much, much more than ambulating calculators. We do what no machine can ever do. We go far beyond just giving a logical or coherent arrangement to a set of data: we give *meaning* to the information that reaches us. We place it in a moral and ethical framework, we measure its aesthetic worth, we search for its spiritual value. We relate all that we see, hear, feel, to the mysterious entity we call the *self*. What is this *self*? It is more than the body, more than the mind, more than a collection of genes, beyond the reach of any chemical or physical analysis. Yet there is nothing more real, nor more important to us. One can easily track the path by which a computer processes information. But when one tries to track how the eye sees a tree, how the mind pictures it, how the heart responds to it, how the self relates to that tree and places it in a limitless expanse of time and space, the path vanishes into a misty infinity. No laboratory technique will ever map the distant contours of that path nor trace it to its end. In the darkness only one light shines - the ineffable biblical declaration that we are *made in the image of God*.

THE PARADOX OF SCIENCE

Most people think that a good scientist is someone who discards all pre-conceived ideas, strips out all prejudice, and approaches research with a determination to follow the path of truth wherever it may lead. Such a person has no place for dogma, no tolerance for willful blindness, finds it inexcusable to ignore clear data or put aside plain evidence, and resists any interference by outside authority.

Unhappily perhaps, such a person has never existed. Yet that image is the one that gives moral force to most scientific endeavour. It is the ideal by which they measure themselves and their enterprise, while in practice they must ignore it. As we have seen, all scientists, whether consciously or unconsciously, must work within the framework of the view of things accepted by the larger community, and especially by the community of scientists. Any evidence that contradicts that canon is at worst rejected as false,[82] or at best put to one side in hope that further discoveries will remove the problem. There is nothing else they can do. If science ground to a halt every time some piece of contradictory evidence cropped up nothing would ever be achieved. Scientists, like the rest of us, must proceed on the basis of what they know, not what they don't know or can't answer.

---

[82] As for example, when scientists who are committed to the view that the cosmos is a closed system, not susceptible to divine interference, simply refuse to consider any evidence of a miracle. Within their community the view prevails that miracles are impossible, therefore any supposed "evidence" of one must be spurious. But the same rule applies, albeit in different areas, to every group of scientists.

So here is a paradox: the scientific enterprise can succeed only by ignoring one of the major premises upon which it is based: its objectivity and neutrality! Scientific success depends upon a selective, even prejudiced, use of the available evidence. But that ought not to surprise us, for it simply mirrors the paradox that is threaded through all of life. Which brings us to

FACT VERSUS THEORY

You should recognise the difference between scientific *theory* and genuine *fact*. Evolution, for example, may be based upon certain observed facts, yet it is only one of several different ways to explain those facts. So while it may be reasonable to say that the biblical book of "Genesis" does not belong in a biology class, neither does any attempt to teach Evolution as if it were an indisputable *fact*. Darwin's theory may be dominant at the present time, but its foundations are under assault even by some scientists, and it may eventually be cast onto the scrap heap of history. That is particularly true when Evolution is turned into a theory of *origins* (rather than a theory of biological development).

Here, for example, is one major problem that has never been satisfactorily answered by evolutionists. Many features of life, both plant and animal, are useful only in their present fully developed form; no intermediate stage of development would have offered the creature any benefit. Therefore, in the struggle for "survival of the fittest", those features, since they brought no advantage, would have been discarded.

I have read somewhere that Darwin himself once said that to suppose "the eye could have been formed by natural selection seems, I freely confess, absurd to the highest degree." Absurd for two reasons: *(1)* there is no imaginable process by which some impersonal force could have invented an intricate marvel like the eye; and *(2)* since an eye remains useless until it is perfect, under the evolutionary theory of natural selection it should have been sloughed off long before it could begin to function. Hence the eye is impossible. Yet you have two of them that serve you well! As a theory of origins Evolution has serious deficiencies.

So learn to distinguish fact from theory. Fact we must endorse. Theory we are completely free to reject.

THE BOUNDARIES OF SCIENCE

Science that truly deserves the name will admit things it can never know beyond doubt. The "truth" claimed by science represents not certainties but only probabilities. "Scientific" truth can never be final nor absolute; it is always open to question and modification. This is another of the paradoxes that beset the scientific method. No statement can be considered "scientific" unless it *is* open to question and to possible falsification. This is the difference between a scientific statement and a statement of opinion. Suppose I say, "Oh, what a beautiful cloud formation!" That is not a "scientific" statement, for there is no objective way to make it true or false. It is true for me; but it may be false for another. It remains only my opinion. But if I say, "All sand is white," then that *is* a scientific statement, because it can be falsified. But now here is the real paradox: <u>*every* scientific statement must be, and eventually will be, either modified or falsified.</u> Why? Because new findings continually make old ones obsolete. Today's verities become tomorrow's crudities. Final truth, absolute truth, will never come from a scientific formula!

So then, what is reckoned to be "true" in science is actually true only in two ways:

> ➤ it represents the highest level of mathematical or experimental probability the scientist is presently able to attain; and

> ➤ it conforms to the conventions of the scientific milieu that is presently dominant.

That is, out of many possible ways of explaining natural phenomena, this "truth" is the one most acceptable within our present culture. There is no such thing as objective, dispassionate, scientific discovery, simply because there is no such thing as an objective, dispassionate scientist. Every researcher brings to the task a particular pair of eyes and a certain way of thinking. Each has a bias that makes him or her more disposed to be convinced by some proofs than by others. Each carries a package of personal, philosophical, and cultural conditionings that cannot be discarded or even ignored. This hidden inner bent irresistibly shapes not only what the researcher sees and does, but *how* it is seen and done, and *why*. It predisposes every scientist to reach certain conclusions in preference to others.[83]

An example of this process can be seen in the way people glean quite diverse meanings from books they read, or from political statements, or from a piece of poetry. Some are conservative, some are liberal, some are free-thinkers, others depend upon authority. How different we all are! Who can ever say that his or her reading is the final, the only correct, one? So with our reading of the Book of Nature, except that here the wisest and best among us must reckon themselves scarcely literate. Carlyle recognised this 150 years ago -

> "We speak of the Volume of Nature: and truly a Volume it is, - whose Author and Writer is God. To read it! Dost thou, does man, so much as well know the Alphabet thereof? With its Words, Sentences, and grand descriptive Pages, poetical and philosophical, spread out through Solar Systems, and Thousands of Years, we shall not try thee. It is a Volume written in celestial hieroglyphics, in the true

---

[83] I might add that, happily or unhappily, the same set of blinkers sits over the eyes of the interpreter who opens the Bible, and endeavours to formulate from its pages theological truth!

Sacred-writing; of which even Prophets are happy that they can read here a line and there a line. As for your Institutes, and Academies of Science, they strive bravely; and, from amid the thick-crowded, inextricably intertwisted hieroglyphic writing, pick out, by dexterous combination, some Letters in the vulgar Character, and there from put together this and the other economic Recipe, of high avail in Practice. That nature is more than some boundless Volume of such Recipes, or huge, well-nigh inexhaustible Domestic-Cookery Book, of which the whole secret will in this way one day evolve itself, the fewest dream!"[84]

Remarkably, one and a half centuries later, there are still some who think of nature as an open book whose secrets must all one day be known, and whose purpose will be made clear. But there are growing numbers of scientists (many more than Carlyle's "fewest"), both agnostic and Christian, who are willing to admit the severe limits imposed upon what they can learn by using the methods of science. Let me suggest three of those limits -

THE ORIGIN OF THINGS

No matter how they speculate about the matter, nor what theories they devise, nor how close their theories approximate the truth, there is no way for scientists to know beyond doubt how the universe came into being -

"In point of fact, the philosophers admit that the first principles of all things are indemonstrable. So that if there is a demonstration at all, there is an absolute necessity that there be something that is self-evident, which is called primary and indemon-

---

[84] Op. cit., Book Three, Chapter Eight; pg. 194.

strable. Consequently, all demonstration is traced to indemonstrable faith."[85]

"The most striking fact that science has discovered is that there was a beginning to the universe, because the inability to determine the cause of that beginning means that there are limits to the powers of scientific enquiry. That's a very open-ended situation, and it paves the way to a dialogue. If science does not have the last word, then the word of others is more acceptable."[86]

THE MEANING OF THINGS

A physicist trying to find the meaning and purpose of the universe by penetrating the physical world down to the level of electrons is looking in the wrong place for an answer he cannot find. One might as well try to find the meaning of this page of print by dissecting it into all its parts - the ingredients in the ink, the chemicals and fibers in the paper, and so on. Such an enterprise must fail before it has begun. If you don't know the language, then you can't read the book, and taking it apart with a pair of scissors won't help you!

But there is one certain way to learn the truth: ask the author to explain his book to you! We need the Word compiled by God to explain the World created by God.

By definition, science is the study of nature, and especially of those parts of nature *(1)* that are subject to analysis; *(2)* that occur regularly; and *(3)* that can be reduced to a repeatable experiment. How then can a science so defined reasonably pass judgment on

> ➢ the existence of God (who lies outside nature), or

---

[85] Clement of Alexandria (c. 200), in "Stromata" 8:3. The same opinion was held by Plato, Aristotle, and others.

[86] Robert Jastrow, op. cit.

- ➤ on the occurrence of miracles (which are not regular), or
- ➤ on the existence of purpose (which cannot be physically analysed), or
- ➤ on the resurrection of Christ (which is unrepeatable)?

Science can tell us much about the "what" and "how" of things; it cannot possibly tell us "why" - for that is locked in the mind of the Almighty.

THE END OF THINGS

We have seen that science is unable to demonstrate the *ultimate* cause of anything. It can speak only in terms of *possibilities, probabilities,* and *statistics.* It can finally say no more than "this is the way it has always happened, so presumably it will continue to do so."

Likewise, there are limits to what science can say is possible in the future - e.g., can such a miracle happen; will the world be judged by God? To such questions the scientist, as a scientist, can give no proper answer -

> "(The virgin birth) is a story that purports to tell us how the birth of Jesus came about. From a scientific, biological, standpoint, the virgin birth seems impossible. *Science is based on observation.* The most that a true scientist can say about the virgin birth is this: 'I do not know of any instance where it has occurred.' What he *cannot* say is: 'There can be no virgin birth.' For him to make the latter statement would be to get outside the realm of science and into the realm of the metaphysical. The scientist has no business going from science to metaphysics without telling his listeners what he has done. He has ceased being a scientist as soon as he gets into metaphysics...

> "Moreover, the virgin birth involves the miraculous. Once miracles are denied, then, of course, the virgin birth becomes an impossibility. But even here the scientist can do no more than say, 'I do not know of any evidence to support miracles.' He cannot say that miracles are impossible without getting out of science and into metaphysics."[87]

Note the statement: *"science is based on observation."* That must always be remembered. For there are many things that cannot be observed, including both the beginning of all things and their eventual end. On those two questions the scientist has two choices: *agnosticism*, or *faith*. Does that make agnosticism a better choice? No, because as we have seen, even the agnostic cannot function unless he adopts without proof certain *"self-evident"* propositions (which themselves were not thought to be self-evident until the message of the Bible was finally understood and believed.)

By any measure, then, the Christian perspective seems to be the more rational. At least, no one can sensibly accuse it of being irrational, or contrary to the facts.

WONDER AND FAITH

Alongside all the wizardry and technology of our modern society, two attributes of a humble spirit remain essential -

WONDER

> "I remember a clear morning in the Ninth Month, when it had been raining all night. Despite the bright sun, dew was still dripping from the chrysanthemums in the garden. On the bamboo fences and crisscross hedges I saw tatters of spider webs; and where the threads were broken the

---

[87] Harold Lindsell, The Battle For The Bible, pg. 155.

raindrops hung on them like strings of white pearls. I was greatly moved and delighted. As it became sunnier, the dew gradually vanished from the clover and the other plants where it had lain so heavily; the branches began to stir, then suddenly sprang up of their own accord. Later I described to people how beautiful it all was. What most impressed me was that they were not at all impressed."[88]

> Pity the man or woman who has lost the capacity for wonder, who passes by the mystery and beauty that everywhere abounds without noticing or caring. How much better the attitude of the psalmist -

"O Lord, our Lord, how majestic is your name in all the earth! ... I look at the heavens above, made by your hand, and at the moon and the stars, which you have fixed in place, and I say, 'Who am I that you should take any notice of me, or my people that you should care about us?'" (Ps 8:1, 3-4).

Then again, what astronomer has ever managed to surpass the simple beauty captured by Jane Taylor in what some have called the world's best-known and most-translated poem -

> Twinkle, twinkle, little star,
> How I wonder what you are!
> Up above the world so high,
> Like a diamond in the sky.

---

[88] The Pillow Book Of Sei Shonagon; tr. by Ivan Morris; Penguin Classics, 1967; Selection # 84, pg. 148. Sei Shonagon was a lady-in-waiting to the Empress, at the Japanese imperial court, c. 985. Her father was a provincial official, but is best known as a poet and scholar, traits his daughter emulated. Nothing is known of her life after her term of court service ended.

> When the blazing sun is gone,
> When he nothing shines upon,
> Then you show your little light,
> Twinkle, twinkle, all the night.
>
> Then the trav'ller in the dark,
> Thanks you for your tiny spark.
> He could not see which way to go,
> If you did not twinkle so.
>
> In the dark blue sky you keep,
> And often through my curtains peep,
> For you never shut your eye
> Till the sun is in the sky.
>
> As your bright and tiny spark
> Lights the trav'ller in the dark,
> Though I know not what you are,
> Twinkle, twinkle, little star![89]

Long after the ponderous tomes of some modern astronomers have been forgotten, long after their theories have been tossed with laughter into the rubbish bin, Jane Taylor's lines will still be sung around the world, and simple people will wonder about the mystery of the starry skies.

FAITH

The secular mind, which accepts no evidence save that supplied by human reason, or that can be verified by experience, remains coldly unresponsive to biblical testimony. But faith brings its own evidence, faith conveys its own witness, faith authenticates itself within the believer, unlocking an understanding that surpasses what the eye alone can see or the flesh experience. When doubt looks at

---

[89] First published in 1804, and since then translated into numerous languages, to be recited by millions of children around the world.

the scriptures it can see nothing more than the fallible writings of men. But when faith looks at that same word, divine light strikes the sacred page, and faith at once perceives that this is indeed the reliable word of God.

"By faith we <u>know</u>!" cried the apostle (He 11:3). That indeed is a revolutionary concept. It cuts right across the materialism and pretended rationalism of this world. The scriptures insist that the answer to the most fundamental questions ("Where did it all begin, why is it here, how will it end?") can be found only by the proper use of faith.

Now let me close by returning to the sense of wonder, and a final passage by the great Scottish critic -

> "(A true philosopher) insists upon the necessity and high worth of universal Wonder; which he holds to be the only reasonable temper for the denizens of so singular a Planet as ours. 'Wonder,' says he, 'is the basis of Worship: the reign of Wonder is perennial, indestructible in Man; ... ' That progress of Science, which is to destroy Wonder, and in its stead substitute Mensuration and Numeration, finds small favour (with the true philosopher). ...
>
> "Above all, that class of 'Logic-choppers, and treble-pipe Scoffers, and professed enemies to Wonder; who, in these days, so numerously patrol as night-constables about the Mechanic's Institute[90] of Science, and cackle, like true Old-Roman geese and goslings about their Capitol[91], on any alarm, or on none; nay, who often, as illuminated Skeptics, walk

---

[90] Familiar in the 19th century as meeting places for scientific discourse and debate.

[91] Legend has it that in the days of Old Rome the city was saved from an attack at night when the invaders disturbed a flock of geese, whose loud cackles warned the defenders.

abroad into peaceable society, in full daylight, with rattle and lantern[92], and insist on guiding you and guarding you therewith, though the Sun is shining, and the street populous with mere justice-loving men': that whole class is inexpressibly wearisome to him.

"Hear with what uncommon animation he perorates: 'The man who cannot wonder, who does not habitually wonder (and worship), were he President of innumerable Royal Societies, and carried ... the epitome of all Laboratories and Observatories with their results, in his single head, - is but a Pair of Spectacles behind which there is no Eye.' Let those who have Eyes look through him, then he may be useful."[93]

Neither science nor faith should close the door against each other. Let both speak where they are competent to speak. Let both be gently silent where they have no competence. Let both stand in awe before the splendour of the Creator and his marvelous works.

---

[92] As night-watchmen used to do in the times before cities were illuminated at night.
[93] Thomas Carlyle, op. cit. Book I, Chapter 10.

100

ADDENDA

IS THERE AN OBJECTIVE REALITY?

Does the world exist as an objective reality, independent of any observer? Is the moon there only when I look at it? The question seems absurd, yet some of the discoveries in the fields of relativity *and* quantum physics *suggest the opposite. Space and time have been shown to be interchangeable, or (more strongly), not separate entities at all, but one indivisible unit, which could be called "spacetime". Einstein demonstrated how one observer might see the entity as space, while another would see it as time, and that they would be unable to agree on what they had observed.*

A simple (and limited) illustration of this may be found in the different worlds seen by different artists. Ask a group of skilled artists to paint a particular tree, and the results will be startlingly different - all the way from a near-photographic portrayal to a swirling abstraction. The differences between them are more than just differences of skill, but more fundamentally, of perception. *Or consider again the world seen by the colour-blind. Which is the* real world - the one I see, or the one they see?

In the sub-atomic world, electrons, the constituents of an atom, show the characteristics both of a particle and of a wave - that is, they can be seen as individual objects (like a collection of little pebbles rolling along), or like a wave of the sea, which is a movement on the surface of the ocean rather than a separate entity. Which aspect electrons present depends upon how they are being measured, or even observed. So, are they objects or wave motion? There is no way to fix the answer, except to say that the ultimate building block of the universe is apparently a piece of pure information, with no tangible material reality at all. That piece of information has the potential to resolve itself into many different forms, but which potential is realised is strongly influenced, if not absolutely determined, by the observer.

This is a baffling mystery to the physicists. At the time of this writing, they are unable to explain the meaning of what they observe. Accordingly, there are two schools of thought -

THE RELATIVISTS

There are those who argue that there is no such thing as an *objective reality,* independent of the observer. The only reason it is there, is because you perceive it! In the expression of Niels Bohr*: "there is no deep reality underlying the world of phenomena."* It is in fact the act of observation, of "measurement" that calls the phenomenon into existence.

To express it differently: the world is not made out of ordinary objects possessing tangible attributes. Such reality as may exist is created only within the consciousness of the observer. Why then do we all observe (nearly) the same thing? Only because we are somehow "coded" genetically to have a similar consciousness.

What we call physical *reality* comes into existence only when the processed "information" about an observation enters into someone's mind. At that moment, what was formerly just a mathematical equation, a mere potential, coalesces into the substantial environment we experience day by day.

So the entire universe is composed of unrealised *potentiality,* until in the instant of observation it is transformed into the world of realised *actuality.* But that actuality endures only a moment before it decays into mere memory - and vanishes forever!

In this view, then, atoms are not actually "things"; they are rather an imaginative construction of the observer, and have no existence apart from the observer.

If we find it difficult to accept that the real world is not real, it is because we lack any language that can adequately explain the atomic environment. Therefore we are unable to imagine a universe composed of pure potential, one that lacks any substance until it is decoded by a conscious mind.

THE REALISTS

Contrary to the relativists, there are others who argue that objective reality does and must exist independently of any observer. This claim obviously accords with our everyday experience. The mysteries (it is said) that the relativists build their case on, would vanish if we had better knowledge, or better ways to explain what we observe. Indeed, referring back to the passage quoted above from *Through the Looking Glass*, we might say that the nonsense of saying that there is an objective reality is "as sensible as a dictionary" compared with the nonsense of saying that there is no objective reality!

On the whole problem of quantum reality, and our perception of it, Casti makes the following observation -

> "(Whatever) position you care to hold, the experimental data will not refute you. As it turns out, *each* of the above positions is in complete accord with the experimental evidence! So until there's an experimental breakthrough of some kind, the position you hold on the quantum reality issue is more like a religious conviction than a matter of science."

So then let no scientist accuse us Christians of wandering in a wilderness of unsupported faith!

PARADOX

Consider these two statements -

"Don't read anything on this page!"
"You must ignore this sentence."

What can you do with them? They lock you into an unresolvable dilemma. To heed them, you must do the very thing they tell you not to do. The only escape is to turn away from them. Thus the world has paradox at its root, which cannot be controlled except by stepping out of the system altogether.

Here are some more paradoxes -[94]

Add to the Liar's Paradox of Epimenides (mentioned above) an earlier version put by Eubulides (Greek philosopher, circa 350 B.C.), "If I am lying, am I telling the truth?"

Eubulides suggested another paradox: if one has a grain of sand and one adds another grain of sand, one does not have a pile of sand. If one adds one more grain one still does not have a pile. So if by adding one grain at a time to what one has, one still does not have a pile, then one can never have a pile of sand.

Try this one: "The next sentence is a lie. The first sentence is true."

If in this village the Barber shaves all those in the village who do not shave themselves, who shaves the Barber?

---

[94] None of these paradoxes are my own invention. I confess that I am not clever enough to do so. They have been gleaned over the years from various sources.

A traveler is walking to a specific location. First he walks half the distance, then half the remaining distance, then half of that distance. As the traveler continues he will always have half the remaining distance to travel and so will never reach his destination.

Here is one from Don Quixote. This paradox was mischievously set up to confuse the chevalier's servant Sancho. A great lord built a bridge across a river to give access to his estate. At the end of the bridge he built a gallows. Everyone crossing the bridge had to say where they were going and why. Those who answered truthfully were allowed to pass. Those who answered falsely were hanged. One day a man walked over the bridge and declared that he had come to die on the gallows. What were the judges to do? They said: "If we let this man pass freely he will have sworn a false oath and, according to the law, he must die; but he swore that he was going to die on the gallows, and if we hang him that will be the truth, so by the same law he should go free." Sancho found a cunning way out of the dilemma, but you will have to read the book to learn what he said.[95]

Zeno of Elea (490-430 B.C.) propounded a number of paradoxes which demonstrated logically that there is no such thing as space, and nothing can be divided into smaller parts. Space and divisibility are logical absurdities, yet we all experience them every day! He showed also that time is contradictory, by a paradox which proved that double a period of time is also equal to its half. In another puzzle, Zeno argued that a flying arrow is logically impossible. If the arrow is moving it must either be moving in a place where it is, or in a place where it is not. It cannot be moving in a place where it is, or it would not be there; and it cannot be

---

[95] Miguel Cervantes, Don Qixote; tr. J. M. Cohen, Penguin Books, 1956; pg. 798-799.

moving in a place where it is not, for it is not there. So then, where is it?

You would find a description of Zeno's paradoxes in any good encyclopaedia.

In the same encyclopaedia, you should read the article on the Indian philosopher Nagarjuna (100-200), who in a series of astonishing "proofs" demonstrated that nothing is real: causation is impossible; change cannot happen; matter has no existence; time is illusory; space is a myth; and the like! All of which we *know* is crazy, yet no one, by logical argument alone, can prove him wrong!

Russell's Paradox: A set is either a member of itself or not a member of itself. To a set which does not contain itself as a member, give the name regular. For example, the set of people does not include itself as a member, since it is not a person. Then to a set which does contain itself as a member, give the name irregular. An example is the set of sets with more than, say, five elements. Now, is the set of all regular sets regular or irregular? If it is regular, it cannot contain itself. But it is the set of all regular sets, thus it must contain all regular sets, namely itself. If it contains itself, it is irregular. If it is irregular, it contains itself as a member, but it is supposed to contain only regular sets. This paradox was particularly devastating to Gottlob Frege a German mathematician. He had just finished the second volume on the logical development of arithmetic. The appendix of his second volume begins "A scientist can hardly encounter anything more undesirable than to have the foundation collapse just as the work is finished. I was put in this position by a letter from Bertrand Russell ... "

And for those with a mathematical bent, here is a logical algebraic formula that proves 1=2. There are many other similar mathematical paradoxes -

If a=b, then 1=2.

$a = b$ then

$a^2 = ab$ then

$a^2 - b^2 = ab - b^2$ then

$(a^2-b^2)/(a-b) = (ab-b^2)/(a-b)$ then

$(a-b)(a+b)/(a-b) = b(a-b)/(a-b)$ then

$a + b = b$ then

$a + a = a$ then

$2a = a$ therefore

$2 = 1$ or $1 = 2$.

Faced with such imponderables, what is left but to trust the testimony of scripture that the universe is real, it was created by God, and will fulfil his purpose!

CAN YOU BELIEVE YOUR EYES?

The picture on the other side of this page illustrates how your mind must sift out the chaos of information that reaches it through your eyes. Can you trust what you see? That depends upon how your mind goes to work! At first sight, the picture is nothing but random marks. But look again! It actually contains a three-dimensional, stepped image of the name "JESUS", floating in mid-air, and rising out of a multi-layered oval frame. There are at least eight layers of depth in the picture! To see it, follow these instructions -

(1) Stare at the space between the two dots, and diverge your eyes inward until the two dots become three. If necessary, move the sheet backward and forward a little until you see the three dots. Focus on the middle dot (which should look blacker and sharper than the others). After a few moments you should see a three-dimensional image beginning to appear on the mottled screen below. The effect is astonishing!

(2) Once the image has appeared, you should be able to keep it in focus, and to look straight at it. As your eye becomes accustomed to it, the image will grow in clarity. Some people see the image in a few seconds, others may take several minutes, or even longer; but since the image is based upon optical laws (not a trick), if you persevere you should be able to see it.

(3) If you have trouble focusing on the dots, hold the sheet against your nose, stare between the dots, and then move the sheet slowly away until the three dots form. If you still can't do it, show the picture to some friends. One of them may see the image easily, and then be able to help you.

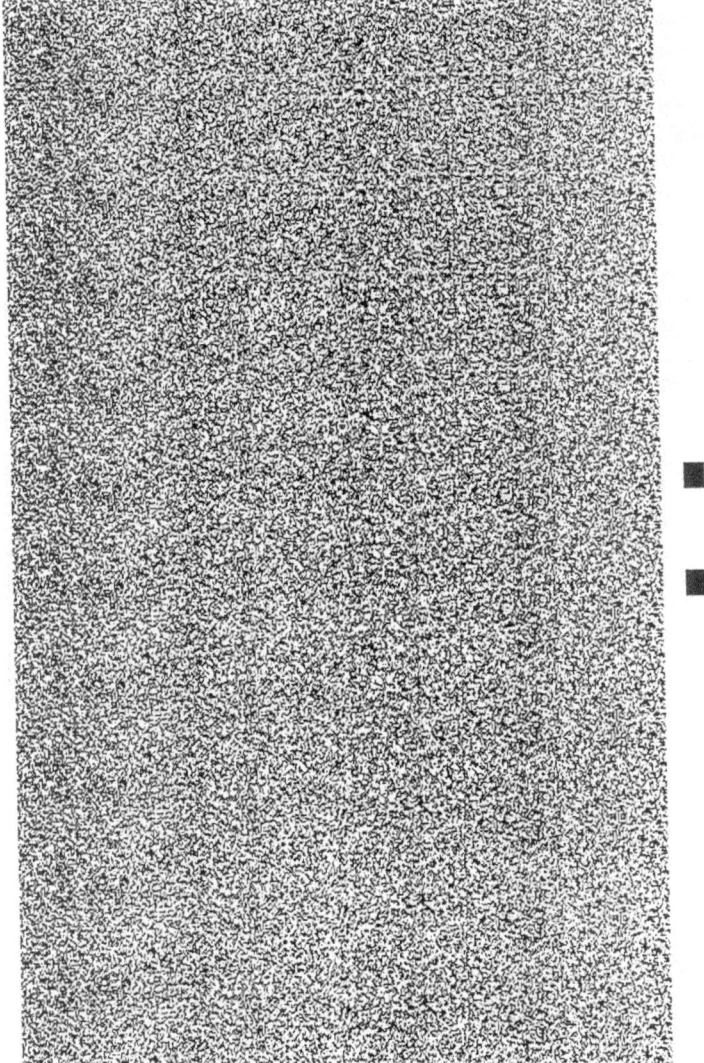

110

PART TWO

THE PROOFS OF GOD

Chapter Five

THE SOUL'S LEFT HAND

Madam,

Reason is our soul's left hand, Faith her right,
   By these we reach divinity, that's you;
Their loves, who have the blessing of your sight,
Grew from their reason, mine from fair faith grew.

   But as, although a squint lefthandedness
Be ungracious, yet we cannot want that hand,
   So would I, not to increase, but to express
     My faith, as I believe, so understand ...

But soon, the reasons why you are loved by all,
   Grow infinite, and so pass reason's reach,
Then back again to implicit faith I fall,
And rest on what the catholic voice doth teach;

   That you are good: and not one heretic
     Denies it: if he did, yet you are so.[96]

In those lines John Donne expresses his admiration of a noble lady, the Countess of Bedford. But he does so by the striking poetic device of likening his confidence in her to his trust in God, declaring that his love for God does not spring from sight, but from faith. Others may argue their way to God, but he prefers the beauty that faith alone uncovers. At best, he says, human reason is an awkward, squint-eyed, left-handed guide. Not that he scorns reason. If he had only a

---

[96] John Donne (1572-1631), "To the Countess of Bedford", stanzas 1,2,4,5a.

clumsy left hand, would he part with it? Neither will he part with reason. Nonetheless, it cannot guide him toward an *increase* of faith, but only to a better *understanding* of it. For in the end, faith reaches far beyond reason's bounds, and knows, though all the world may deny it, that God is there, and that he is good.

Now that is where we stand. Although the following chapters examine various "proofs" of God, and therefore depend upon logical persuasion, let us at once admit the limits of the enterprise. Useful as logic may be, it must remain only "the soul's left hand". Those who are argued into belief in God can be argued out of it. Either we "know by faith", or we shall never know at all. After all, anyone who bothers to produce rational arguments for the existence of God must already believe in God, and therefore has no need of the arguments! Accordingly, whether or not God can be "proved" by reason alone, I believe already, and therefore know him. He was undeniably real to me long before I knew there were such things as intelligent grounds for faith.

Does that make belief irrational, a thing of blind prejudice? Of course not. Faith cannot survive in an environment of *un*-reason. What is contrary to good sense, or against rational thought, is equally antagonistic to sound faith.

Nor does faith lack all rational evidence. There are abundant reasons to believe in God. The open eye sees God in the sky above and in the earth around; the sensitive heart feels him in the depths of its being; the responsive spirit communes with him each day. When a believer prays and heaven answers, God becomes as authentic as life itself!

If someone creeps up behind me in the dark and strikes me with a stick, I certainly know he was there. I may never see him, nor learn his name, nor have any other contact with him, but I cannot doubt his reality! No clever argument could give me any stronger evidence of his existence than my bruise; nor could any wise philosopher persuade me that my assailant did not exist! Similarly, I am a man struck by God. Not all the thinkers in the world could convince me that he is a figment of my imagination. The marks left by his hand are on my soul!

JUST A GIANT FRAUD?

Someone may now say that religion is nothing more than personal opinion, a thing of subjective feelings. How do I *know* that my experience of God is not a delusion? I suppose in the same way that I *know* my memories of the past 60 years are not a delusion but pictures of what actually happened. Yet I cannot rationally substantiate those memories. For all I know, everything that now is, including all that I remember, may have sprung into being only a few minutes ago, with each item looking as old or as young as the illusion requires[97]. Cannot a forger build evidence of antiquity into a freshly made pot? So the universe may be just one gigantic fraud.

"What nonsense!" you reply, and quite rightly. Yet you cannot, by logical argument alone, *prove* the contrary. Rather, you just *know* that the suggestion of fraud is silly. In the same way, although my sense of God's presence in my life, both yesterday and today, may be a delusion, I find it vastly more reasonable to accept the evidence as true. That is not unreasonable, for human society worldwide depends upon axioms that cannot be proved, and therefore must be accepted on trust -

AXIOMS WITHOUT PROOF

Some people are prone to argue that one should not believe anything except upon sufficient evidence, nor should one believe more strongly than the evidence requires; and on both counts (they say) theism fails. Such claims are sensible

---

[97] This puzzle was first presented by Bertrand Russell.

only on the surface. They collapse before one strong defence: *no statement can be proved without using propositions that are unproved.* That is, only by calling upon axioms whose truth everyone simply accepts can anyone *prove* the truth of any other statement. All knowledge, in fact, is built (and can only be built) upon the prior admission of a set of ungrounded axioms. Take this very basic example. Suppose I want to prove that the world around me is real, and exists independently of my perception of it. I can start to work on such a proof only by using evidence which must pre-suppose that the world *does* exist. So I cannot prove by pure reason *alone* that all those objects I see out there are real. Shall I then doubt their existence? That would be stupid. The "proof" that they are there rises up within me and is too overwhelming to deny. I cannot accept that my senses of sight, touch, hearing, smell, are fraudulent.

Consider also the other side of the cosmos, the microscopic. No one has ever *seen* an electron, or is ever likely to. Scientists can do no more than observe what they take to be evidence of the presence and activity of electrons. Therefore the concept of electrons is an hypothesis developed by physicists to explain certain phenomena. The concept may be highly probable, but that does not alter its theoretical nature. Yet who would intelligently deny what the physicist propounds?

Now it seems to me that the kind of evidence a physicist depends upon to establish his argument about electrons is exactly what I depend upon when I affirm God. Divine activity is the best hypothesis to explain what happens to me day by day.

Yet God, of course, is more than just an hypothesis. Far more strongly than any physicist may "feel" the reality of electrons, the sense of God overwhelms my soul. I am like the Psalmist, who observed the starry heavens and cried out that his ear was deafened by their loud telling of the glory of

God. Even if I wished to do so, I could no more tear out of my heart its sense of the Creator's wisdom and power than I could banish from it all knowledge of the world around me.

Think also about the mathematician's world. Beyond question, every mathematician must use prior rules, which are not susceptible to rational proof. Does lack of proof invalidate those rules? No, for without them the entire system would collapse. Successful calculations depend upon their wise use. How then, since we can't "prove" them, do we know, that those axioms are *true*? If not by reason, then certainty must come from some other way of "knowing", one that is above reason. It must also be more reliable than reason, for it speaks when reason is dumb. But surely, if we can trust this mysterious inner sense to lead us to mathematical truth, may we not trust it also to lead us to God? At least everyone should admit that a believing heart can gain the same assurance of God's reality, and gain it in the same way, as a mathematician does when he asserts the unfounded principles upon which his own dogma must stand. Rational evidence is not the only way to unassailable knowledge.

A LEAP OF FAITH

What about the other argument, that belief should not rise above the strength of the evidence? If we allowed ourselves to be confined by that rule we would never discover anything. I showed you in the first part of this book that every single scientific proposition that has ever been adopted as truth depends upon a jump from limited proof to a final conclusion. The evidence is *never* enough to fix any proposition as undeniably true. A certain amount of data is gathered - sometimes more than others - and the researcher then takes an intuitive leap into a comprehensive theory of what he has observed. If he jumps in the right direction, then his experiment will be repeatable, and its results will find a useful place in society. But the hiatus between mere probability and final proof is one that science must always cross upon the bridge of faith.

Every day we take for granted a thousand things that either cannot be proved at all, or must stand upon inadequate proof - if by "proof" you mean unassailable logical demonstration. In fact nothing in the world has ever had an absolute underpinning. We are obliged to believe a multitude of things that have at best only limited proof.

So then let us cast off once and for all the naive idea that science is able to produce all the evidence we need about everything that matters. On the really important issues science tells us nothing at all; and on the rest, its evidence always remains partial. Why? Because pressed too far, any quest for knowledge ends in confusion, especially when one is searching for *ultimate* knowledge. Plutarch recognised this limitation long ago -

> "If you apply the whole force of your mind in your desire to apprehend (Being), it is like the violent grasping of water, which by squeezing and compression loses the handful enclosed, as it spurts through the fingers."[98]

Inherent limitations are built into the human mind. How can a finite tool ever expect to comprehend the infinite? We can learn much; but we cannot learn all.

ALPHA AND OMEGA

We have now come this far: I *know* God is there, even if rigorous logical proof cannot be constructed. But suppose inarguable evidence *did* exist, what then? I would still not place too much reliance upon it, for I could not allow that God is nothing more than the conclusion to a philosopher's debate. Knowledge does not *end* with God, it *begins* with

---

[98] I have lost the source of this quote.

him. Until I know God, I know nothing, nor is anything worth knowing without the knowledge of God. He is the *Alpha* and the *Omega* of all that is true. Yet between the beginning and the end there is much that is worthy. As the poet recognised, reason can be employed as an adjunct to faith. Reason can at least demonstrate that faith is *reasonable*. It can help us to understand why we believe. It can strengthen us against the attacks of enemies.

So let us start our examination of the rational evidence for God's existence. The technical name for this quest is *"natural religion"*, which distinguishes it from the *"revealed religion"* found in the Bible.

To the biblical authors, of course, such a quest would have seemed absurd -

> *"Only fools say to themselves, 'There is no God'"* (Ps 14:1; 53:1; and see also 19:1; Ro 1:18-20).

Among the ancient Hebrews the first proposition of scripture (Ge 1:1) was so self-evident that only people who had lost their senses could doubt or deny it. Even in his deepest misery, Job never thought to question God's existence. But we *find ourselves alive during an age where, for the first time in history, masses of people scorn the knowledge of God. Therefore it is useful to demonstrate that our faith does not stand on airy clouds of religious superstition, but has a foundation of good reason.*

HOW DO WE KNOW THAT GOD EXISTS?

ATHEISM VERSUS THEISM

Atheism and theism both begin with a supposition about God. One says, "There is a God;" and the other, "There is no God." But neither of those propositions is open to strict logical demonstration. God cannot be proved, like some kind of algebraic formula. The opening statements of both theism and atheism are assertions that one either accepts or rejects. The question is, how can you tell which of them to choose? Obviously, you must decide which one of them fits the evidence better than the other. My intention is to show that the most rational choice is the theistic position. But I cannot deny that uncertainty will remain, a gulf that faith alone can bridge. Why is that so? Because dubiety resides in the very nature of the question and of the evidence. Consider the following example. For any logical argument to be successful, three things are usually necessary:

1. a set of true premises;
2. a valid conclusion; and
3. a willingness to be convinced.

With that in mind, it is possible to present three kinds of structured argument, or syllogisms (as they are called), each consisting of a major *premise,* a minor *premise, and a* conclusion. *The first kind fails; the second is true; the third is probable, but can be doubted:*

- a syllogism based on false premises, which must therefore lead to a false conclusion: "If pink cats exist, so do green dogs. Pink cats exist. Therefore green dogs exist."
- a syllogism based on true premises, which leads to a conclusion no reasonable critic will deny: "All people get hungry. I am a person. Therefore I get hungry."
- a syllogism that may seem to be true in its premises and its conclusions, but which for various reasons some people may refuse to accept: "The virtuous are more happy than the corrupt. I am virtuous; my neighbour is corrupt. Therefore my happiness is greater than his."

The proofs of God's existence are not like the first syllogism (based on falsehood), nor like the second (based on certainty), but more like the third: convincing to most people, but not so convincing that they cannot be rejected by those who think they have reason to do so. This then is our position: while we cannot prove the existence of God beyond all possible doubt, we can certainly demonstrate two things: belief in God is not irrational; and there are excellent reasons for theism.

Indeed, we can show that for people without prejudice, the available proof makes it more rational to accept God's existence than to *reject it*. Actually, that is not surprising. Insofar as proof is possible for any matter, it is easier to prove a positive statement than a negative one. Remember again the illustration of the sandy beach. I need only one footprint to show that a person once stood in that place; but to prove that no one has ever walked there, I would have to know its entire history from the beginning of time. Likewise, it is not difficult to gather evidence of God's existence, to point to his footprints upon the sands of time; but to prove that God does not exist I would need a level of knowledge that only God can possess!

FOUR DIFFERENT APPROACHES

I said above that one of the necessities for a successful syllogism is willingness on the part of the hearer to be convinced. If someone has already made up his or her mind not to believe, then no proof will convince them, not matter how rational or incontestable it may be. There are four kinds of mind that are not open to any proof that God exists -

1. THE NATURAL MIND

"Those who cling to a natural mind cannot grasp the things that belong to God" (1 Co 2:14).

Science, since it focuses on investigating natural phenomena, inevitably follows a naturalistic approach to interpreting its collected data. That is as it should be. Science behaving responsibly will stay within the confines of its own lore. A problem arises however when scientists topple over the edge into *naturalism*; that is, when they try to use science to answer questions it cannot even reasonably *ask* let alone *solve*. There may be no room for the Bible in the laboratory; but neither does the test tube belong in the pulpit. Science deals with *effects*; it cannot solve the riddle of *causes*.

Similarly, because scientists must deal with material things, there is always a temptation for them to fall into *materialism*, to believe that matter is all that exists, and is its own cause. Yet no scientist (speaking as a *scientist*) has any competence to judge whether or not there is a spiritual dimension, or a human soul, or survival after death, or an eternal Creator. When people lapse from science into *scientism* they should be honest enough to say so. They have shifted from the bench to the pulpit; natural research has suddenly become philosophical speculation. An example occurs when the teaching of evolution (as a description of process) is turned into *evolutionism* (a theory of origins). When those changes happen, the scientist has turned prophet and become the promulgator of a new religion. He is of course entitled to his opinion and to speak out. But he ought not to do it in disguise, still wearing his laboratory coat. Let him put on a cleric's garb and declare honestly what he is about.

2. THE VEILED MIND

Some scientists hope that by analysing the constituent parts of the physical world, tracing each chemical or nuclear path back to its tiniest component, finding out how everything works, they will solve the riddle of life and remove the need for God. But that notion contains an absurdity almost beyond excuse. Here, say, is sponge cake. Dissect it down to molecular level. You will learn much about the "how" and the "what" of the cake. But will you know anything about the "where" or the "why"? *Where* did this cake come from? *Why* is it here? *Where* is it going? Why this kind of cake, and not another? Why this shape, and not another? Why here, and not somewhere else? Suppose the cake is a two-layered vanilla cream sponge, that I had purchased for a child's birthday party. How could any physical, chemical, nuclear, philosophical, or any other kind of analysis tell you those things? I am the only who knows *why* I had it made.

Science is adequate to answer many questions, and its answers are amazingly brilliant and wondrously useful. But there are questions I feel constrained to ask that no scientist will ever be able either to answer, or even hazard a reasonable guess. Yet those are the most important questions! So let science continue to give sensible answers to the questions it is qualified both to ask and to answer. But it must stand humbly mute before the most pressing concerns: who am I; why am I here; where am I going? The naturalistic methods of science cannot even begin to solve such intangible mysteries.

3. THE UNBELIEVING MIND

See John 3:3; Hebrews 11:6. The Bible teaches that "unbelief" is not a state of neutrality, but rather of deliberate rejection of the truth. The natural state of men and women is one of *faith*. Anyone *open* to believe will be drawn to faith by the Holy Spirit. It takes a considerable act of will to squash all instinct toward faith in God and to adopt a determined agnostic or atheistic stance.

Let me illustrate that by considering the idea of "truth". Some secular scientists are prone to think that their researches will disclose the "truth" about the world, from the outer reaches of the macrocosmic to the inner recesses of the microcosmic. But what is "truth"? Is it a property of material things, or does it lie altogether beyond them? Even asking the question should be enough to evoke an immediate response that truth cannot lie in the world of objects. Truth is not something you can dissect with a scalpel, or weigh in a balance, or reduce to a formula. It is an ethical concept. It has nothing to do with how molecules behave in a crucible.

The idea of "truth" presupposes the existence of a moral standard that stands outside the material realm. How can it be otherwise? If a higher dimension does not exist, if matter is all that there is, then everything, including life, is nothing more than action and reaction among clusters of atoms. Our thoughts, feelings, beliefs, choices, become mere mechanical responses to an interplay of molecules. Our mental processes would then not differ significantly from any other electrical or chemical routine. They would be akin to taking two clear liquids and mixing them together to produce a reaction that turns the fluid red. The redness cannot be called true, or moral, or good, or bad, or right, or wrong, or anything else except inevitable. But if I reject that mechanical view of life, and insist that my thoughts are my own, and that they are true, not false, then at once I remove them from the control of mindless atoms. I lift them above the confines of matter. I am consciously or unconsciously measuring them against a separate ethical standard, one that has neither origin nor restraint in the physical world.

So then, anyone who claims to know the real "truth" about anything, reveals by that very claim the existence of a dimension beyond the perimeter of laboratory experiments. Truth and falsehood have no meaning for an atom, which lacks any power of choice and simply follows the dictates of natural law. Ethical values lie beyond the scope of physical objects. Scientists, therefore, who hope to discover the "truth" by analysing matter are like a man looking for Sydney in Spain - he is lost before his journey begins!

4. THE FOOLISH MIND

We are back now where we started: the Bible offers no proof of God's existence, because it everywhere assumes that God is, and denounces as "foolish" anyone unwise enough to deny it

> "It is a remarkable fact that none of the canonical writers ever employed nature to prove God. They all endeavour only to bring their hearers to trust in him who is already known to exist. David, Solomon, and the rest, never said: 'There is no void, therefore there is a God.' They must have had more knowledge than the most learned men who came after them, all of whom have used that argument. This is highly significant." [99]

Martin Luther had a similar opinion -

> "Now if someone wants to say that God is not God, just let him go. For we have nothing to do with the man who believes nothing at all and denies everything one says of God and God's word. So they also teach in the schools[100], (that any person) who dares deny what nature teaches everyone and what is granted by the reason and intellect of all men should not be disputed with, but should be referred to a physician, who should clean out his brains for him."[101]

WHO NEEDS PROOF?

Seldom have the proofs of God ever led anyone to faith in Christ. Have they then no value? Some scholars have indeed denied them any usefulness. But that seems needlessly harsh, for there are two groups of people who gain

---

[99] Blaise Pascal (1623-62), Pensees, # 19, slightly paraphrased; tr. John Warrington; J. M. Dent & Sons Ltd, London; 1973.

[100] That is, the secular schools and universities, not just the theological seminaries. Atheists were still rare in the 16th & 17th centuries. The situation today would have been unimaginable to a Luther or a Pascal.

[101] What Luther Says; compiled by E. M. Plass; Concordia Publishing House, 1959; Vol 2, pg 538.

substantial benefit from rational arguments in favour of faith -

THE BELIEVER

Here is a strange fact: many people do not doubt the existence of God until *after* they become Christians! How can that be? Simply because they now begin to establish a relationship with the Father and to expect great things from him. All is well so long as the relationship is working, and good things are happening. But then comes a time when the Lord seems to withdraw his presence, when prayer is not answered, when unrighteousness crushes righteousness, when darkness seems to prevail over light. Doubts assault the believer's mind. Perhaps God is not there after all? Perhaps all those spiritual experiences were a delusion, and answered prayer a mere coincidence?

At such times the proofs of God's existence can become very encouraging to struggling faith. Indeed, true faith always develops into a blending of heart and mind, of soul and reason. Jesus said that we must worship not just in *spirit*, nor just with *truth*, but with both spirit *and* truth (Jn 4:23-24). Nor should intelligence merely act as faith's helper, but must be a vital part of belief. The central truths of religion should flow into every aspect of our lives, just as the centre of a circle flows into every radius and out to the circumference.

This union of reason with belief is not a new idea. John Donne, in his poem *Honour Is So Sublime Perfection* argued 300 years ago that intelligent thought cannot be separated from religious faith -

> ... discretion
> Must not grudge zeal a place, nor yet keep none,
> Not banish itself, nor religion.

> Discretion is a wise man's soul, and so
> Religion is a Christian's, and you know
> How these are one, her *yea*, is not her *no*.
>
> Nor may we hope to solder still and knit
> These two, and dare to break them; nor must wit
> Be colleague[102] to religion, but be it.
>
> In these poor types of God (round circles) so
> Religion's types, the pieceless centres flow,
> And are in all the lines which all ways go.

And again from Blaise Pascal -

> "If we submit everything to reason, there will be nothing mysterious or supernatural about our religion. But if we offend against the principles of reason, our religion will be absurd and ridiculous."[103]

You may have no need of the proofs of God *today*, but you may find them very helpful *tomorrow*!

The second person who may find in these proofs an encouragement to faith is

THE SINCERE SEEKER

Well-presented arguments can encourage faith in those who desire to believe, but whose minds have been shaken by the attacks of infidels. This book, for example, may be the very thing you could put into the hands of an enquiring friend, someone who is disposed to believe in God, but needs first to see that faith does not require him or her to abandon rational thought.

---

[102] That is, reason must not be merely a help to faith, but inseparably united with it.

[103] Op. cit. # 358.

THE REAL NATURE OF THESE PROOFS

Our goal is not the defensive one of trying to justify our faith in God by frantically searching for evidence of his existence. Rather, our approach is positive. We follow the method used by science: given the fact of the world around us, let us now seek out the most reasonable explanation for its existence, and for our own presence here. Several hypotheses are available. Among them is *theism*, which believes both that God exists and that he maintains an active involvement in human affairs. Our task is to show that theism is the most reasonable explanation of the available data. While leading you in this quest I will have to engage you in some vigorous reasoning. That can be a perilous enterprise. Reason has its uses; it also has its limits. So before we begin, let me close this chapter with some further admonitions against putting too much weight upon reason -

> "There are two extremes: to exclude reason; to admit nothing but reason ... Faith tells us plainly what the senses do not tell us, but not the contrary of what the senses perceive. It is above the senses, not opposed to them ... The final step taken by reason is to acknowledge that there is an infinity of things beyond its grasp; it is indeed weak if it cannot go as far as to understand that. And if natural things are beyond its grasp, what shall we say of supernatural things!"[104]

---

[104] Pascal, op. cit. #368, 370, 373.

Chapter Six

THE ARGUMENT FROM DESIGN

Since the time of the ancient Greek philosophers, the proofs of God have fallen into 5 groups. Each of these groups has had times of eminence and of disgrace. The current position is one of cautious acceptance, while acknowledging that they all fall short of an absolute demonstration.

To philosophers, logical demonstrations have value only when they are exhaustively argued; whereupon they tend to be debated out of existence. They become so obscure, so tortuous, that to anyone except another philosopher they are meaningless. I am neither a philosopher, nor the son of one (if I may paraphrase Amos), so the following pages will not try to walk the labyrinthian paths that savants delight to tread. For a plain man, plain evidence will be the most convincing. Once again, Pascal strikes to the heart of the matter -

> "All our reasoning amounts to no more than giving way to feeling ... One man says that my feeling is fancy, another that his fancy is feeling. We need some rule. Reason offers itself as such; but reason can be made to serve any purpose, and hence there is no rule ... The metaphysical proofs of God are so remote from human reasoning, and so complicated, that they make little impression. If some find them profitable, it is only during the moment that they grasp them; an hour afterwards they fear they have been mistaken!"[105]

---

[105] Op. cit., # 2, 38. See also the Addendum that follows this chapter.

How true that is! As often as I have written about, or taught on, the proofs of God, they have seemed strong only while I was discussing them. An hour later, the sound of one child laughing carries more weight than a thousand scholarly dissertations!

If you have done any reading in philosophy, you will have been struck by the realisation that almost every premise put forward by one thinker is demolished by another! Why can't they agree? Because there is an imperfection in the human mind, which means it is ultimately unable to arrive at truth by its own unaided efforts. Far from strenuous mental effort being a guarantee of truth, whenever human thought is pressed too far it always ends in ambiguity. Here is a simple example. Think about the universe. In imagination begin to travel across the galaxies. Continue on toward the outermost limits of the starry heavens. Eventually you will reach the last fragment of rock in the last galaxy. You are at the very end of the created world. What then? What lies yonder?

When your mind tries to grasp what exists beyond the edge of everything, it falters, it falls apart, it pulls back from the unfathomable precipice.

So God has placed limits upon human achievement. Whenever men and women press beyond those limits, the confusion of Babel is repeated. Which means that faith alone is the final key to truth.

Nonetheless, the classic proofs of God, if they are dealt with plainly, do provide for most people sufficient evidence of God's existence. So let us look at the first of them-

THE TELEOLOGICAL ARGUMENT

In the beginning, God created everything,
And he fixed their boundaries for ever.
He arranged all his works into proper order,
And he set their elements for all time.

> They never become hungry, or weary;
> They never abandon their appointed tasks;
> They do not trespass upon each other's place;
> They never disobey the command of the Lord.
> Then the Lord looked down upon the earth,
> And he filled it with good things.[106]

"He arranged all his works into proper order." That is what we mean by the *teleological* argument - a name that comes from the Greek word for "design". Everywhere one looks there is evidence of conscious *design* in the world. Across the centuries many renowned thinkers have reckoned this the most compelling of all the proofs.[107] The ancient Greek philosopher Plato (428-348) was the first one to present this argument coherently. After him came many other sages who drew attention to the regular succession of the seasons, the majestic march of the planets, the exquisite crystalline snowflake, the delicate beauty of an orchid, and a thousand other obvious signs of order in the universe. Today, scholars might prefer to look into the extraordinary ecological balance that holds all life together in harmony. Just a small disruption in the chain of dependence can be enough to destroy several species that stand higher in the chain. Can this congruence of relationship and dependence be only the result of an accident? Can it be nothing more than a coincidence of mindless forces? I could more easily believe that an earthquake built Sydney!

Suppose you were to take a group of counters, numbered 1-10, and throw them into the air. What likelihood is there they will fall in a straight line, and in their correct sequence? If you saw them so arranged, you would take it for granted

---

[106] Sir 16:26-30a.

[107] For example, among many others: Plotinus; Telesio; Newton; Paley; Voltaire; Mill; Tennant. (From the Dictionary of Philosophy & Religion

that some intelligent agent had done so. Could you *prove* that? No, for it is certainly *possible*, from the point of view of pure reason, for a group of counters to fall *accidentally* into a straight line and in numerical sequence - but you could never bring yourself to believe it had actually happened! The odds against it are just too enormous. You would simply *know* that some hand had arranged them so neatly. I feel the same way when I see a lovely rose, or a baby's tiny hand.

William Paley[108] was the first person to use the illustration of finding a watch in a field, and concluding that it must have been made by a watchmaker. What other conclusion would be possible? Paley applied the same argument to a telescope, and from there to the human eye. Any sensible person, looking at a telescope, would at once conclude that it was conceived and crafted by a skilled maker, and that it was designed to suit the human eye. Said Paley, *"There is precisely the same proof that the eye was made for vision as there is that the telescope was made for assisting it."*

Holmes Rolston[109] put it this way: "Like the man who survives execution by a 1000-gun firing squad, we are entitled to suspect that there is some reason we are here, that perhaps there is a "Friend behind the blast." Then he lists a number of the fine-tuned values, the fragile nuances of nature, that are essential for the universe to be as it is. Here are some of the matters he raises -

(1) At the moment of the creation of the universe, if the force of attraction between the protons in a hydrogen atom had been only slightly different, nothing would have emerged - no galaxies, no planets, no life.

---

[108] William Paley. In his <u>Natural Theology</u>, published in 1802.

[109] Professor of Philosophy at Colorado Sate University, in an article "Shaken Atheism: A Look at the Fine-Tuned Universe", "Christianity Today", Dec. 3rd, 1986; pg. 1093.

(2) A variation of just one half of one per cent in a certain atomic level would have banished carbon from the universe, and life as we know it would not exist.

(3) Far from being extravagantly large, recent research has shown that just for life to come into being and to flourish on our own single planet the universe must be as old, vast, and diffuse as it is. Reduce the universe to half its present size and "it would run through its entire cycle of expansion and recontraction in about one year"!

(4) The density of the matter scattered across the galaxies has also been shown to be just right. Any heavier, and the whole would long since have collapsed together. Any lighter, and it would have all been flung into vaporous mists.

(5) The expansion rate of the universe is exactly right to maintain a proper temperature level on Earth. Any faster or slower, and life would be impossible. Alter the electrical charge in various sub-nuclear particles by the tiniest fraction, and the entire chemistry of the universe would change radically. Stars would burn out. Galaxies would whirl into rapid oblivion. Instead, everything is in exact proportion to maintain the starry heavens above us, and the green earth around us. Even the Earth is just the right size, "near the geometric mean of the size of the known universe and the size of the atom." Change these proportions only slightly and everything that is familiar would vanish. Nothing would be the same.

So from protons to planets, from grains to galaxies, the universe everywhere shows signs of a constraining hand. Certain chemical values were set and maintained, nuclear forces were proportioned and balanced, all exactly right for maintaining the existing order and for allowing life to continue. There are only three possible ways to explain this seeming design, this ecological and natural pattern, this apparent purpose that holds all things together -

THE RESULT OF ACCIDENT AND EVOLUTION

Some scholars argue that the existence of order and balance in the universe can be explained by natural forces alone. To infer God from the structure and harmony of the world (they say), it must first be shown that this could not have occurred without divine intervention. After all, were the pattern of things *not* workable, the system would have failed long ago. It is a tautology to say that the world functions because it is functional. It could not be anything else, for otherwise it would simply not be here! Since everything *is* here, it is just the inevitable result of the right conditions happening to come together. Now that may be logically true, yet it still runs counter to our ordinary instincts. Few people can cheerfully accept the pronouncement of, say, Bertrand Russell, in his dismissal of the teleological argument -

> "If you accept the ordinary laws of science, you have to suppose that human life and life in general on this planet will die out in due course: it is a stage in the decay of the solar system; at a certain stage of decay you get the sort of conditions of temperature and so forth which are suitable to protoplasm, and there is life for a short time in the life of the whole solar system. You see in the moon the sort of thing to which the earth is tending - something dead, cold, lifeless."[110]

Lord Russell thought it was "nonsense" for anyone to feel depressed by the prospect of a "dead, cold, lifeless" future, although he was at least willing to allow that it was a "gloomy view". Few would quarrel with the latter opinion. And few could be happy with the idea that in the end everything is worthless, without purpose, without meaning, having no goal but utter annihilation. Across the ages there has rather been

---

[110] *Why I Am Not A Christian*, Unwin Books, London, 1975; pg. 18.

a sense that we cannot be fully human if we succumb to a sense of meaninglessness, or of absurdity. Ordinary people find it impossible to accept that chaos is truly the ultimate reality, and darkness the only end. The structures of human society, our instinct toward purposeful organisation, the useful arrangement of our daily activities, are not just matters of practical necessity. They seem to reflect a deeper affirmation of, and to result from, our sense of the rationality and order of the universe. So said the pagan Roman emperor who has been called "one of the noblest men in history", Marcus Aurelius (121-180) -

> "Either a universe that is all order, or else a farrago thrown together at random yet somehow forming a universe. But can there be some measure of order subsisting in yourself, and at the same time disorder in the greater Whole? And that, too, when oneness of feeling exists between all the parts of nature, in spite of their divergence and dispersion?[111] ... Either the world is a mere hotch-potch of random cohesions and dispersions, or else it is a unity of order and providence. If the former, why wish to survive in such a purposeless and chaotic confusion; why care about anything, save the manner of the ultimate return to dust; why trouble my head at all, since, do what I will, dispersion must overtake me sooner or later? But if the contrary be true, then I do reverence, I stand firmly, and I put my trust in the directing Power."[112]

Against such claims, however, an atheist might point to the abundant evidence of *disorder*: the savage facts of crime, war, and disease; the prosperity of the undeserving, the

---

[111] <u>Meditations</u>, Book Four, #27; tr. Maxwell Staniforth; Penguin Books, 1986; pg. 69.

[112] Ibid. Book Six, #10; pg. 92.

misery of the worthy; and ultimately, the obscenity of *death*. If there is an almighty deity, why does the world continue to carry so much pain? How much power can God *really* have, if he is unable to bring his own creation under control?

That argument is so superficial one could hardly treat it seriously, had it not been raised by some truly brilliant thinkers (among them Bertrand Russell). So we reply that the only disordered thing in God's world is fallen humanity, and those parts of the creation affected by human wrongdoing. Can God be blamed for that? Only if you think he should rob you of your freedom of choice. But if you and I want to remain free moral agents (and who does not?), then we must accept the consequences, for good and ill alike.

Robert Browning, in his poem *Bishop Blougram's Apology* explores the above ideas. The bishop is debating with an infidel, and he admits that sometimes he doubts his own doctrines, and that there are mysteries he cannot solve. The infidel at once mocks the bishop's lack of fixed and exclusive faith, and declares him a hypocrite. Undismayed, Bishop Blougram in turn challenges the stability of the infidel's unbelief, which is wracked by the very doubts that trouble a Christian's faith. The bishop then bids both himself and his opponent to begin afresh by rejecting all dogma -

" ... our dogmas then
With both of us, though in unlike degree,
Missing full credence - overboard with them!
I mean to meet you on your own premise:
Good, there go mine in company with yours!

And now what are we? Unbelievers both,
Calm and complete, determinately fixed
Today, tomorrow, and forever, pray?
You'll guarantee me that? Not so, I think!

> In no wise! All we've gained is, that belief,
> As unbelief before, shakes us by fits,
> Confounds us like its predecessor. Where's
> The gain? How can we guard our unbelief,
> Make it bear fruit to us? The problem's here.
> Just when we are safest, there's a sunset touch,
>
> A fancy from a flower-bell, some one's death,
> A chorus-ending from Euripides, -
> And that's enough for fifty hopes and fears
> As old and at once as nature's self,
>
> To rap and knock and enter in our soul ...
> All we have gained then by our unbelief
> Is a life full of doubt diversified by faith,
> For one of faith diversified by doubt! ... "

Here then is the issue: which would you prefer, a life of doubt troubled by occasional urges toward faith, or a life of faith, troubled by occasional urges toward doubt? Says the bishop, quite sensibly, the second choice is not only more conducive to contentment, but is also more rational!

And if we still cry out for a clearer sign? We are not left in ignorance, for into humanity's struggle to find a solution to the dilemma of suffering, to hold onto a sense that life *does* have meaning, comes the revelation of scripture. Not that the Bible solves every mystery. It does not. But where silence still prevails, scripture provides a way to face the darkness with courage and faith.

Second, we could say that the evidence of order and purpose in the universe is

THE RESULT OF CONSCIOUS DESIGN

> "The more that physicists find out about the universe, the more improbable it becomes. Take the amount of electron charge in an electron and the ratio of the masses of electrons and protons. If these

> values had been slightly different - as, for all man now knows, they could have been - there would not have been any stars of the right sort to permit the development of life ... (Some argue) that the universe had no choice but to develop in a way that would ultimately allow observers to exist. (But) this is ... incredible ... "[113]

Let us return to Professor Rolston's illustration: if 1000 marksmen were to shoot at you from a close distance, you would be highly astonished to observe yourself still alive. How did they all miss? Could it have been mere accident? Was it an outworking of inevitable natural law? Neither explanation would be credible to you. You would surely cast around for some other explanation, associated with conscious purpose. If you are still alive after facing the firing squad, then someone must have arranged for every soldier to aim away from you. Similarly, few people can believe that by mere accident, or by mindless forces, life has survived the multitude of perils that should so easily have destroyed it. Our presence on earth is more incredible than escaping a thousand sharpshooters. Too incredible to have happened of its own accord. Somewhere there is a guiding hand.

From a similar argument, Dr William Craig of the Catholic University of Louvain concludes -

> "(Likewise) man should be surprised - and so should look for deeper explanations of the fact - that he observes features of the universe which are both improbable and necessary conditions of his own existence."[114]

Some have argued that our present universe is just one of a long succession of random universes, each one born out of

---

[113] I have lost the source of this quote.
[114] From an article in <u>The Economist</u>, March 11, 1989, pg 90.

the other, in an endless cycle (the explosion-contraction, or *Big Bang*, theory). They claim that just as a long series of dice throws will eventually, and inevitably, turn up a double-six, so a long series of universes will sooner or later produce one that is capable of creating and supporting life.

But Dr. Ian Hacking of Toronto University claims that such arguments rest on a "muddle about probability." It is true that a long series of dice casts must eventually produce a double-six; but it is equally true that a double-six may result from the *very first* throw.[115] In other words, the showing of a double-six is by itself no proof at all that there has been more than a single throw. Hence -

> "the idea that there have been many randomly different universes does not make *this* universe any less improbable, and so does not help to explain it. Cosmologists unwilling to accept their own improbability had better come up with some better explanations."[116]

It is true, of course, that rigorous logical proof of conscious design is not possible; but that kind of proof is absent from a host of things that we take for granted. Our natural instinct is toward assuming that the degree of order in the universe, and its suitability for human life and happiness, is the work of a Designer. How else can we explain why so much of the world is so lovely in form, and why this beauty often seems to have nothing other than an aesthetic value? The sense of mystery, awe, and wonder that fills us when we contemplate the universe is not satisfied by naturalistic assumptions -

---

[115] Indeed, no matter how many times the dice are cast, the probability of a double-six occurring on any one throw always remains exactly 1 in 36. Gamblers who believe otherwise will soon be poor!

[116] Op. cit.

> "Two things fill the mind with ever-increasing wonder and awe, the more often and the more intensely the mind of thought is drawn to them: the starry heavens above me and the moral law within me."[117]

We cannot believe that men and women are in the end nothing more than "a fleeting organic excrescence on the surface of single planet of a minor star out on the periphery of a medium-sized galaxy"![118]

A COMBINATION OF BOTH

The most probable explanation for the mixture of order and disorder in the universe is a combination of the two previous ideas. That is, God has created the heavens and the earth for a purpose; but because that purpose permits a large measure of free choice and behaviour, some anarchy can result. Think about a school playground. The yard is bounded by its fence, and adult teachers hover in the background, yet the children rush around pellmell, flowing in and out of various activities, playing, fighting, laughing, weeping. Order and disorder evident together.

Suppose we do accept that there are many marks of *design* in the universe, what then? We must at once accept also the idea of *purpose*. Would you build a house, and then ask what use you can make of it? Evidence of design is also evidence of purpose. And if there is a purpose behind the universe, then it must arise from a *conscious* decision, for there can be no such thing as an unconscious *purpose*. Design requires a designer; purpose demands a purposer. Furthermore, purpose and design must be *premeditated*;

---

[117] Immanuel Kant, in the concluding words of his Critique Of Pure Reason (written in 1781).

[118] J. H. Hick, "Arguments For The Existence Of God"; McMillan Press, London, 1979; pg 35.

hence, the Designer existed before anything else, and must be at least the *Architect* of all things, if not their actual Builder. Who is that Architect? The *teleological argument* cannot by itself lead to the Christian God, for a finite and imperfect universe cannot be made the proof of an infinite and perfect God. After all, the universe might be the product of eons of trial and error by a host of deities. But at least we can say that the evidence *does* point to the existence of a great *Intelligence* prior to the beginning of the universe.

CONCLUSION

What have we found so far? The connectedness, the balance, the interplay, the mutual dependence, of the multitudinous forces that work together to give coherence and orderly function to every part of the universe provide clear evidence of intentional design. This design is so complex that disturbance of just one element could wreck the whole. The odds against everything happening by mere accident, and not by intention, are immeasurable.

There was also a second problem: not so much what is *here*, but what is *not* here. Why this world and not another? Why this set of natural "laws" and not another? Out of the stupendous number of possible cosmic variations, why the only one that is suited to the arrival of life? Could blind, impersonal, non-living chance have given rise to living, seeing, intelligent persons? It is easier by far to believe in God.

No one has expressed the teleological proof more lyrically than the 5th century Greek orator, St John Chrysostom -

> "Could so many good things, tell me, arise of themselves? The daily light? The beautiful order and the forethought that exist in all things? The mazy dances of the stars? The equable course of nights and days? The regular gradations of nature in vegetables, and animals, and people?

Who, tell me, is it that ordereth these? If there were no superintendent Being, but all things combined together of themselves, who then was it that made this vault revolve, so beautiful, so vast, I mean the sky, and set it upon the earth, nay, more, upon the waters? Who is it that gives the fruitful seasons? Who implanted so great power in seeds and vegetables?

"That which is accidental is necessarily disorderly; whereas that which is orderly implies design. For which, tell me, of the things around us that are accidental, is not full of great disorder, and of great tumult and confusion? Nor do I speak of things accidental only, but of those also which imply some agent, but an unskilful agent. For example, let there be timber and stone, and let there be lime withal; and let a man unskilled in building take them, and begin building, and set hard to work; will he not spoil and destroy everything?

Again, take a vessel without a pilot, containing everything which a vessel ought to contain, without a shipwright; I do not say that it is unequipped and unfinished, but though well equipped, it will not be able to sail. ...

"In fine, if we chose to follow out the argument of providence, both generally and in detail, time itself would fail us. For I will now ask him who would start those questions above-mentioned, are these things the result of providence, or of the want of providence? And if he shall say, that they are not from providence, then again I will ask, how then did they arise? But no, he will never be able to give any account at all. And dost thou not know that?"[119]

---

[119] From "Homily XIX" on Ephesians 5:15-17; <u>Nicene and Post-Nicene Fathers</u> Vol. XIII, ed. Philip Schaff; Eerdmans Pub Co reprint, 1979; pg. 140. John is reputed to have been the greatest of all the Greek preachers; hence the appellation "Chrysostom", which means "Golden Voice".

ADDENDUM

PASCAL'S WAGER

In a famous passage in the *Pensees*, Blaise Pascal presented a "wager" which he thought should force faith in God. Here is a summary of his argument, from an article in the *Dictionary of Philosophy and Religion* -

> "Noting that proofs of God are convincing at most only in the moment of their demonstration, [120]Pascal suggests that a rational approach to God leads one either to atheism or to deism.[121] No wonder, since one is attempting to reach by reason the infinitely incomprehensible. But there *is* a way to use reason to prepare the way for God. Is it worth one's while, in terms of the mathematics of probability, to gamble on religious faith? Addressed to his sceptical and freethinking friends, some of whom were enthusiastic gamblers, *Pascal's Wager*, as it has come to be known, answers this question.
>
> "The conditions are that one is already involved in the wager.
>
> "To believe or not believe in God's existence is actually to wager that he exists or does not exist. If we believe he exists, and he does, the reward is eternal happiness. If we believe God exists, and he

---

[120] See the quote from the "Pensees" at the beginning of this chapter.

[121] "Deism" is not the same as "theism". The latter sees God as immanent in human affairs; the former accepts the existence of God, but removes him from any involvement in the affairs of the universe.

doesn't, nothing is really lost, and the same is true if we disbelieve and he doesn't exist. However, if we disbelieve he exists and he does, we are damned for eternity. Thus we have everything to gain and nothing to lose by wagering God exists. On the mathematics of probability alone every gambler should find the wager irresistible.

"This does not imply that Pascal approves the calculating attitude involved in the wager. After the way is cleared, the gambler must learn to abase himself, to 'stupefy' himself, establishing a way of life making appropriate the gift of divine grace, should God will it. The God who is hidden to fallen man is present in the power of grace. This is the God of Abraham, Isaac, and Jacob, not the God of the philosophers."[122]

---

[122] Edited by W. L. Reese; Humanities Press, New Jersey, 1980; pg. 414, 415.

Chapter Seven

THE ARGUMENT FROM EXISTENCE

> "A Dialogue between two Infants in the womb concerning the state of this world, might handsomely illustrate our ignorance of the next, whereof methinks we yet discourse in *Platoes* denne, and are but *Embryon* Philosophers."[123]

I cannot but agree with the worthy physician, feeling myself indeed to be an "embryon" philosopher, debating in the shadows of a deep cave. But then, so are we all. The wisest see only a little more clearly than the simplest. Not even the cleverest person on earth can *prove* so common a thing as tomorrow's sunrise, nor so unique a thing as his or her own death. No doubt both events will happen; but that is a confidence built out of statistics, not upon pure reason.

So while there are no *flawless* proofs of God available to us, that should not trouble us. As we have seen in earlier chapters, perfect proof exists for *nothing* in the world, only varying degrees of *probability*. Absolute certainty is something that we do not and cannot have. The idea that science provides final knowledge about *anything*, let alone everything, is our very own modern myth, cousin to the fairy tales of the ancients.

One of the major reasons why uncertainty cannot be eradicated is the nature of human reasoning. All arguments

---

[123] Sir Thomas Browne, <u>Hydriotaphia</u>, Chapter Four. "Platoes Denne" is a reference to The Cave Analogy from Plato's "The Republic", VII. The writings of the gracious Sir Thomas Browne have been continuously in print for over 300 years.

are either *inductive* or *deductive*, and both of them fall short of unequivocal proof. *Inductive* reasoning works from the specific to the general - that is, a few examples are applied to the whole, forming a general law from particular instances. *Deductive* reasoning works from the general to the particular - that is, a previously accepted universal principle is applied to a specific case.

If I say, "I have observed 10 cats purring, therefore all cats purr" - that is *induction*. If I say, "All cats purr; this animal is a cat; therefore it too will purr" - that is *deduction*. You will at once notice the circularity of the conclusions, made apparent by the simplicity of the examples. But the same problem exists in all human reasoning. Think too hard, press your enquiry too far, and you will end up either where you started, or lost in a morass of confusion![124] Lewis Carroll[125] caught this perplexing paradox in a nonsense poem found in his novel *Sylvie and Bruno* -

> He thought he saw an Elephant,
> That practised on a fife:
> He looked again, and found it was
> A letter from his wife.
>
> "At length I realise," he said,
> "The bitterness of life!"
> He thought he saw an Argument
> That proved he was the Pope:

---

[124] This very book, along with all others like it, is an example of circular reasoning; for here we are, using logical arguments to "prove" that **all** logical arguments are fallible! A fine paradox! One could keep spinning around forever trying to resolve that verbal dilemma. There is no solution, except to jump off the hurdy-gurdy at some appropriate spot, and let that be the terminal point of your journey.

[125] Lewis Carroll, the pseudonym of the Rev Charles Dodgson (1832-98), author of "Alice in Wonderland" and "Through the Looking Glass".

> He looked again, and found it was
> A Bar of Mottled Soap.
> "A fact so dread," he faintly said,
> "Extinguishes all hope!"[126]

Just so. You think you have an unassailable argument. You press it further. Does it become clearer? No, it begins to change shape, to carry you where you would rather not go. The experience, as Lewis Carroll suggested (and he was himself a skilled logician), can be very bitter for a serious thinker. There are indeed philosophers who have echoed the Gardener's lament: "All hope is extinguished! The only tool available to us, human reason, is inadequate for the discovery of ultimate reality."

Blaise Pascal long ago recognised the same frailty in logic. He understood that the data are never enough to make any inference final. Conclusions based upon inductive reasoning must always fall short of certainty -

> "When we see a constant repetition of a given effect we conclude therefrom a natural necessity; for example, that there will be a tomorrow, etc. But nature often deceives us, and does not obey her own rules."[127]

The problem has been expressed in another way, by saying that *deductive* reasoning is never sure about its *axioms*, while *inductive* reasoning is never sure about its *conclusions*. Look again at the examples above. The axiom "all cats purr" may be true, but it cannot be altogether proved without perfect knowledge of every feline that has ever existed or ever will exist. Likewise, because ten cats are known to purr, it is indeed highly probable that all other cats will also purr.

---

[126] "The Gardener's Song." A stanza from the song appears in successive chapters of the book.

[127] Op. cit. #922.

But immaculate proof of that proposition will never be found in this world.

Science is a mixture of both kinds of reasoning. Its enterprise (as we have seen) is fundamentally based upon deductive use of unproved axioms; while its conclusions depend upon inductive use of experimental data. Which means that what we are pleased to call "knowledge" is in the end only probable belief. Someone has said that in our quest to understand the nature of things "we can only be reasonable, never rational". In the most rigid sense of logical demonstration, truth is not attainable by the unaided human mind. Certainty belongs only to those who are the recipients of divine revelation, which comes to us in scripture. However, natural theology, in common with secular science, must work within the limits imposed upon rational argument by the deficiencies of our minds. Therefore, the classic proofs of God deal with probability, not certainty. Our task is to show that out of various competing postulates, the biblical propositions are easily the best -

> "Such proof as may be had will consist in showing that theism is the most reasonable interpretation of the world of man, and in displaying the accumulative evidence for the assertion ... that the cosmos ... cannot reasonably be ascribed to fortuitousness, but only to design by a supreme mind, which must be intelligent and moral, the ground of the Good, the Beautiful, and the True."[128]

So we come now to the second of the classical proofs, called

---

[128] I have lost the source of this quote.

THE ONTOLOGICAL ARGUMENT

The name "ontological" comes from the Greek word for "being", and philosophers have constructed this argument in various ways; but there are two main forms -

THE *IDEA* OF PERFECTION REQUIRES PERFECTION

Since many things in this world are sufficient in themselves, we feel no need to imagine them in a better or more perfect form, or as having some higher existence. But there are other things that leave us with a haunting sense of disappointment, a feeling that we are dealing with shadows, not substance. They produce in us an urge to look for some ultimate and ideal fulfilment. We could summarise these unfulfilled things under two categories: *reality*, and *values* -

1. REALITY

Gaze around you. We cannot escape a sense that what we see is merely an imperfect expression of an absolute reality. Think about domestic chairs. What an astonishing variety there are: chairs for kitchens, lounges, dining rooms, bedrooms, and other areas of the home. Can you describe a chair? No, for some have legs, and some don't; some are padded and some aren't; others are wide, narrow, high, low, square, rounded, long, short, upright, laid back, and a thousand other shapes. It will probably remain impossible to teach a robot how to recognise every piece of furniture that is a chair, no matter what its shape; yet you would identify them all at once. Why? Because there seems to be implanted within us an innate idea called *chair* against which we measure each object. We have an internal image of an *ideal* chair, a feeling that somewhere the *perfect* chair exists, of which all earthly pieces are but pale reflections.

Now that is a simplistic illustration, which a philosopher could perhaps tear to ribbons. But it is sufficient for our present purpose. It shows that we *do* have this inner sense of perfection against which we judge what we see, and so pronounce the world imperfect. A similar idea occurs in scripture, where Moses was told that his earthly tabernacle was a poor shadow of the ideal and eternal heavenly tabernacle (He 8:5). Nonetheless it had two uses: it brought benefit to the people during their earthly pilgrimage; and it expressed their confidence that one day they would possess the heavenly reality.

So too, we are content to use material things for now, but all the time we are reaching toward perfection, which we know cannot be found here, but must reside in the heavenlies.

2. VALUES

Just as darkness has no meaning except when it is contrasted with light, or as smoothness can be known only against roughness, so most things in life can be grasped only when there is something to measure them by. That is particularly true of the values we hold dear: goodness, beauty, truth, wisdom, and the like. Our notion of these things seems to demand an ultimate, absolute, and perfect realisation. We measure goodness against an ideal of virtue, and beauty against an intuitive model of loveliness. We strain toward that ideal, we yearn to see it. Notice also how speechless science must be in this realm of values. Can science define what is beautiful and what is not? What theorem can explain justice? Will there ever be a formula to tell us when to laugh and when to cry? Out of a test tube can there ever spring a device to reveal the difference between virtue and vice, or to show us what is good? Yet are not any one of these things more precious than the entire collection of scientific theorising and technological gadgetry? Long before science was invented men and women knew the highest joys of beauty, and they will still be laughing and loving long after the last laboratory has crumbled to dust.

There is then nothing "scientific" about this innate sense of ours that there is an imperishable ideal. Nowhere is that more true than of the greatest virtue known to us: *love*. Nothing in the material world can satisfactorily explain the existence of love. All naturalistic explanations fail, because the effect (love) is so much greater than the cause (survival). For the sake of love, and against their own self-interest, people will make the most astonishing sacrifices. Nothing in evolutionary theory is adequate to show either the need for altruistic love, nor its cause. Under a rule of survival of the fittest such self-denying love is not only unnecessary but actually detrimental. Yet we do not resent it as an enemy but recognise it as the noblest part of human character. Much that "evolution" might think essential we could happily cast aside; but this quality, which finds no satisfactory place in any scheme of evolution, we would hold at all cost.

Our daily experience of human love, despite its many shortcomings, conveys to us a sense that it is still an expression of a perfect ideal of love, which we are sure exists somewhere. Furthermore, love cannot exist merely as an abstract idea, a philosophical precept. Perfect Love must spring from the heart of a perfect Lover. A question at once arises: who is this supreme Author of love? The Bible answers: *God is Love*; and he is also the source of all those lesser loves that reflect the divine ideal.

So then, we discover in ourselves this mysterious capacity to visualise perfection, this innate sense of values. How strongly embedded these concepts are! We could not endure the thought that there is not, nor ever will be any discovery of flawless reality or of impeccable virtue. That is why the greatest of the ancient philosophers were convinced, even without scripture, that reason itself demands the existence of an ultimate *reality*, and of the perfection of all *values*.

Even when people are unable to reason the matter out, they continue to look for that ultimate reality and that ideal perfection. Indeed, surely nothing less than such confidence can make endurable the imperfection of all our experiences on earth (Ro 8:18-23; etc.)

There is another example of this principle in our yearning for happiness. What enormous energy we devote to the pursuit of happiness! Yet in the end even the best of our pleasures leave us with a feeling of emptiness. Are we then doomed to endless frustration? Will there never be any true satisfaction, any lasting fulfilment? Or rather, has God made us so that nothing can bring us final contentment except union with him?

THE *IDEA* OF GOD REQUIRES GOD

St. Anselm (who has been called "the ablest and most influential theologian of the eleventh century") was the first man to express this proof of God. Indeed, it has been called "perhaps the most brilliant of all attempts to prove God's existence" - that is, to prove God's existence by the use of reason alone, without any evidence except what pure thought can provide. Anselm declares that he was filled with rapturous joy when this great proof came to him in a flash of inner illumination. In brief, he put forward the proposition: *"God is that than which nothing greater can be conceived."* Anselm was so delighted by this simple concept that he expressed it, not as a formal argument, but rather as a prayer-

> "So true is it that there exists something than which nothing greater is conceivable, that its non-existence is inconceivable: and this thing is Thou, O Lord our God!
>
> "So truly therefore dost Thou exist, O Lord my God, that thy non-existence is inconceivable; and with good reason, for if a man's mind could conceive ought better than Thou, the creature would rise above the Creator and judge him, which is utterly absurd. And in truth, whatever else there be beside

Thee, may be conceived as non-existent. Thou alone, therefore, most truly of all, and therefore most of all, hast existence; because whatever else there is, is not so truly existent, and therefore has less the prerogative of existence."[129]

However, even an atheist can hold the *idea* of "something than which no greater can exist." For him it might be some fantastic object he has imagined; or he might equate the greatest conceivable thing with the physical universe. So the question becomes: is Anselm's proof just a noble idea; or must it have an external reality; and must that reality be God? John Hick gives this answer -

"To exist in reality, as well as in mind, is greater than to exist only in the mind. Therefore, if something exists only in the mind it cannot be that than which no greater can be thought. For we can conceive of something greater than a 'greatest conceivable being' that exists only in the mind, namely, that same thing existing also in reality. Therefore, that than which no greater can be thought cannot exist only in the mind, but must exist in reality as well."[130]

More simply, the argument can be put as follows -

"One who denies the existence of God has not grasped the concept of God. God, as the being than whom a greater cannot be conceived, cannot be conceived not to exist; for if God could be conceived not to exist, it would be possible to conceive of an existing being greater than God; but to conceive of a

---

[129] "Proslogion", iii; taken from Documents of the Christian Church, ed. Henry Bettenson; Oxford University Press, London, 1975; pg. 137.

[130] Op. cit., pg 71

being greater than the being than whom a greater cannot be conceived is a self-contradiction."[131]

More simply still: we can hold to some ideas (say, dragons) without believing them to represent reality; but we cannot hold the idea of *God* without thinking of him as actually existing. Try this experiment: imagine an absolutely perfect being, one greater than any other that can be conceived. It is impossible to think of such a being without affirming that he also exists; for if he did not exist, he would not be absolutely perfect, since existence is part of that perfection. An absolutely perfect being cannot lack anything required for perfection, including existence. But since we *can* logically conceive of a being who possesses all the attributes of perfection (that is, God), then God *must* exist.

Anselm also believed that his argument could lead to some early definitions of the attributes of God, by listing those values it is better to have than not have -

"What goodness, then, could be wanting to the Supreme Good, through which every good exists? Thus You are just, truthful, happy, and whatever is better to be than not to be - for it is better to be just rather than unjust, and happy rather than unhappy."[132]

TWO OBJECTIONS

Two objections have been raised against the *ontological* argument, and indeed, against *all* the proofs of God -

(1) The argument is nothing more than a pile of words, which have no meaning other than what we ourselves give them. In other words, the most that any argument can prove

---

[131] Baker's Dictionary of Theology, pg 244.
[132] Ibid

is that a man is thinking. No human thought can prove the existence of anything outside itself, because we have no way of demonstrating that our thought processes are reliable, nor that they deal with reality.

Now it is true that we cannot prove logically that our minds are trustworthy; yet none of us is willing to doubt that they are. We are confident that our thoughts are generally reliable, and that our words do deal with real things, not just figments of a deluded imagination. We don't *need* any proof of such self-evident propositions; we just *know* that they are true!

(2) The argument assumes that it is better to exist than not to exist; yet that proposition cannot logically be demonstrated.

Once again, we have to yield ground and admit we cannot *prove* that existence is a better state than non-existence; but neither can we be persuaded that it is untrue. That opinion may be sheer prejudice on our part, but we hold to it most tenaciously. None of us prefers non-existence to existence. Not even suicides. Rather they, like we, are not usually seeking obliteration, but instead hoping to enter a better state. Nor could you find many people who at heart do not believe in that better state. We are now alive, and we expect to keep on living, whether in heaven or hell. But if so, then our life must stand independent of our flesh, which means that it must have a source outside the world of material things. What is that source? According to scripture, it came when God breathed into human clay the breath of life.

Chapter Eight

MEN, WOMEN, AND MORALS

Those who believe in God usually do so for one of three reasons -

(1) Subjective: based on our feelings of anxiety and of dependence; our sense of cosmic loneliness; our wonder at the mystery of creation; our intuitive sense of God, or more broadly, our religious instinct.

(2) Historical: based on the witness of scripture; the subsequent history of the Jews and of the church; God's actions in world history and in individual lives.

(3) Experiential: based on the uniqueness of human life, including our moral nature; our personal encounters with God, and our experiences of answered prayer.

For the vast majority of believers, those kinds of informal "proofs" are quite sufficient to justify their faith, and to strengthen it day by day. Perhaps surprisingly they are also the basis for the arguments that philosophers have developed into three additional formal proofs of God. They carry the ponderous names *anthropological, sociological,* and *cosmological,* but the arguments themselves are fascinating. Here we look at the first of those proofs, and the final two in the next chapter -

THE ANTHROPOLOGICAL ARGUMENT

The name of this proof comes from the Greek word for *man* ("anthropos"), hence this argument uses various aspects of human nature to point to the existence of God. The main part of the argument is based upon our sense of *morality*.

Let me illustrate what I mean by a remarkable story, and then some lines from a well-known poem -

CASABIANCA

In the terrible Battle of the Nile (1798) the French flagship *Orient* was commanded by Louis Casabianca. On board among the crew was his 10-year old son, Giacomo. Under a savage battering by English broadsides, the *Orient* caught fire, exploded, and the captain was mortally wounded. Every sailor who could do so fled the ship, except Giacomo, who stayed by the wheel in an effort to help his gallant father. He perished with his father when the ship, furiously burning, plunged beneath the waves. Eye-witness accounts were taken back to England, where the boy's heroism was immortalised in Felicia Hemans' famous poem *Casabianca* -

> The boy stood on the burning deack,
> Whence all but him had fled;
> The flame that lit the battle's wreck
> Shone round him o'er the dead.

- as the scorching flames drew nearer the child called to his father for permission to leave his post, and called again, and yet again; but since the dying captain gave no reply, Giacomo stood firm against the engulfing fire and the terror of battle until

> There came a burst of thunder sound;
> The boy, - Oh! where was *he*?
> Ask of the winds, that far around
> With fragments strewed the sea, -
>
> With shroud and mast and pennon fair,
> That well had borne their part, -

> But the noblest thing that perished there
> Was that young, faithful heart.[133]

Do you admire the brave child? Why do you admire him? If the materialist is right, and we are nothing but dust, with no immortal soul, and if death means absolute extinction for all of us, what value lies in heroism? It defies reason to squander the one and only thing we have, namely, these few years of mortal life. We should more sensibly *"Eat, drink, and be merry, for tomorrow we die!"*[134] But who will agree that there is no useful difference between a hero and a coward? We cannot help feeling that there is a rule higher than personal advantage, that there exists a powerful moral law, one that is-

INTERNAL AND INESCAPABLE

Every normal person has an inbuilt moral consciousness - the voice of conscience - which speaks in every human heart. There are only two possible sources of this inner morality -

IT IS ARBITRARY AND ACCIDENTAL

But if that is so, then moral conduct is no longer imperative, there is no real "right" or "wrong", only what is convenient or inconvenient. Indeed, the fully moral life would become irrational, because doing what is "right" may be contrary to one's personal wellbeing, while doing what is "wrong" may bring abundant benefit. There are many occasions when one could gain an advantage from lying, cheating, or stealing. If the so-called moral law is just a product of social pressures why not seize every possible opportunity for personal gain? It would be madness not to do so; for if there is no God, no

---

[133] First and last two of ten stanzas. <u>Casabianca</u> was first published in 1829.
[134] Ecc 8:15; Is 22:13; 1 Co 15:32.

life after death, no reward or punishment to come, let us get as much as we can now!

Of course, if there really is no objective standard of morality, then such terms as "lying", "cheating", "stealing", become meaningless, or at best they mean only what the community, or even the individual, says they mean. They no longer have any impartial value. Two rules become enough to replace the Ten Commandments and every other moral code: take whatever you want; do whatever you please.

This issue must be faced: no moral code can arise out of atheism. If there is no God, if matter is all that exists, if we are nothing more than an amalgam of chemicals, then "morality" is an empty term. Those who deny God, yet strive to live morally, are acting against their own philosophy. They can offer no rational grounds for the values they hold. Even less can they find any firm basis (except sheer force) to impose those values upon others.

However, few people can accept such a frightening prospect. Most men and women, in every culture, are convinced that the moral law is something independent of the human race, and not subject to willful change. What sensible person could agree with those thoroughgoing rationalists who reckon it is impossible to call *any* action morally wrong? David Hume, for example, reckoned that murder was not wrong, just unpleasant, especially for the victim. At least one must admire their honesty. Having banished God from the universe, they agree that no foundation remains upon which to construct a fixed moral code. Every action becomes now either functional or dysfunctional; but "right" and "wrong" no longer have any place in the moral lexicon. Indeed, the word "morality" itself has no place, unless it is re-defined to mean, not what *ought* to be done, but what is pleasant.

History shows that in the past *every* human society has depended upon religion to validate its moral code. Belief in God (or at least in some heavenly Arbiter) is the root out of which all moral concepts grow. If there is no God, no Absolute, how can there be any rule of life stronger than personal advantage? The strong will then be absolutely free to plunder the weak. Were the pressure of atheists and humanists toward the abolition of religion from our land to succeed, the ethical chaos that would follow is appalling to imagine. Happily, they won't succeed. By the fiat of God, most people are incurably religious, pricked by conscience, and convinced that a moral law exists outside of themselves.

But if the moral code is not a fabrication of our own, devised to suit our own convenience, then we are compelled to say that

IT IS ORDAINED AND UNIVERSAL

By this we mean that the moral law cannot be determined individually, but has universal force; it does not result from purely natural forces, but is built rather into the very structure of the universe. It does not rise out of the physical world, but is imposed upon it.

The presence of this law is marked especially by that strange thing we call "conscience". Here is a puzzle for evolutionists: where did conscience come from? How did such a powerful moral force rise out of mere chemical reactions? After all, conscience does not depend upon personal convenience, for it is often very inconvenient; nor is it necessary for survival, for it often leads to death. Even when people continually violate conscience, its voice persists. Nor is it a product of Christian society, for it is a universal phenomenon, exercising as much pressure in primitive communities as it does in the most sophisticated.[135]

---

[135] Note again the quote from Immanuel Kant, above. The great German philosopher actually rejected all the classical "proofs" of God except this one. But he acclaimed this part of the anthropological argument as undeniable evidence of a moral Deity.

In essence, conscience judges each action against the criterion of "worthy" or "unworthy". Yet the notion of being "worthy" is meaningless unless there is both an ultimate *Standard* and an ultimate *Arbiter*. We find both in God.

INDEPENDENT OF WHIM

We sense that a moral order exists above and apart from the world of nature -

> " ... the moral law cannot be considered part of the scientific universe. It is more than the way nature *is* and more than what men *do*; it is what men *ought* to do, whether they are doing it or not. And since this moral *"ought"* is beyond the world, unlike natural law, it cannot be considered a formal part of the universe. The moral law calls for an explanation beyond the natural world, for it comes from beyond the observable universe."[136]

Although human morality takes different shapes, and is influenced by culture, religion, environment, and other factors, across history ethical thinkers of every race have arrived at a similar set of rules. There have been few departures from the general principles expressed in the Ten Commandments, which themselves are summed up in a principle taught by many philosophers, *"The Golden Rule"* -

> "You must love your neighbour as you love yourself"[137]

> "Do not do to others what you would not want done to yourself"[138]

---

[136] Norman Geisler; but I have lost the source of this passage.
[137] Moses, 15th. cent. B.C. (Le 19:18)
[138] Prince Gautama, the Buddha, 6th. cent. B.C.; Mahabharata XIII. 55711.

"This is the sum of all righteousness: Treat others as you yourself would be treated. What you would not like if it were done to you, do not do to others"[139]

"We should behave toward our friends as we would wish our friends to behave toward us"[140]

"Do not do to others what would make you angry if it were done to you"[141]

"What you do not want done to yourself, do not do to another person"[142]

"What you yourself would hate, do that to no one else"[143]

"Do not to your neighbour what you would not have him do to you. This is the whole Law; the rest is mere commentary."[144]

"Whatever you want people to do for you, that is what you should do for them. This is the whole Law and the Prophets"[145]

"What you hate to suffer, do not do to anyone else"[146]

---

[139] The Chinese philosopher, Confucius, circa. 400 B.C. The Confucian Analects 15:22,23.

[140] The Greek philosopher, Aristotle (384-322 B.C.).

[141] Isocrates, Greek philosopher and moral teacher (circa 350 B.C.)

[142] One of the maxims of the Stoic philosophers (circa 250 B.C.)

[143] Tobit, to his son Tobias (Tobit 4:15, circa 200 B.C.)

[144] Rabbi Hillel, circa 50 B.C. The story goes that an enquirer came to him and insisted that Hillel teach him the entire Torah while he stood upon one foot.

[145] Jesus of Nazareth (Mt 7:12).

[146] Philo, Alexandrian Jewish philosopher, circa 100 A.D.

"What you try to avoid suffering yourself, do not inflict upon others"[147]

"Let the prosperity of your neighbour be as important to you as your own"[148]

"Do as you would be done by"[149]

"The loveliest fairy in the world; and her name is Mrs Doasyouwouldbedoneby"[150]

The *Golden Rule* is an example of the large degree of moral uniformity reached by ethical thinkers from many lands and cultures. To say that this is just a product of the same practical pressures at work in each place hardly seems adequate. We maintain rather that the idea of a moral law did not originate with human thought; it is not based upon personal opinion or interpretation; it is objective, apart from human society, externally mandated, eternal. The moral law existed before we were born; it will continue after we are dead. Its precepts are universally true, applicable as surely in heaven as on earth, and across the span of all the galaxies.

None of that can be true, of course, if God is denied. For without God nothing remains but the physical world. There could then be no spiritual dimension (for spiritual dynamics cannot arise out of matter), and the whole of human religious experience would be both negated and left without explanation. Nor could there be any such thing as morality, for moral law does not cohere in dust (which is all we are without God). If humans are but ambulating atoms then no one can be held responsible for their actions, for clay has no power of moral choice, it simply obeys irresistible natural

---

[147] Epictetus, Greek philosopher, circa 100 A.D.
[148] Rabbi Eliezer.
[149] The Earl of Chesterfield, in a Letter to his son, Oct 9th, 1747.
[150] Charles Kingsley (1819-1875), <u>The Water Babies</u> Ch. Five.

law. All talk about good and evil then becomes meaningless nonsense. Nor could I ever again suppose that I have a "soul", for how could such an ethereal thing belong to something that is nothing more than a collection of chemical compounds? Materialism turns freedom of choice into an empty phrase, and moral responsibility becomes a weird contradiction.

Of course, not even the most avid secularist *really* believes such things, for they continue to live as morally upright as their Christian neighbours. Yet their commitment to ethical behaviour negates the very philosophy they profess. If we are nothing but accidentally energised earth, born without purpose, living without destiny, in a world utterly ruled by natural law, then there is no point to anything except grabbing all you can while you can. The finest philanthropist has no more real value, nor deserves any better praise, than the most greedy thief. Good people stand no higher than criminals, the cruel are kin to the kind, sloth and labour are equally meritorious. Are they not all products of forces over which they have no more control than a tree does, or a cat, or a beetle?

Even talk about rational "thought" becomes nonsense, for matter cannot "think"; it simply reacts to chemical or nuclear processes. If we are nothing but a concoction of molecules, then what we call "thoughts" are only electrical impulses generated by chemical interaction in the brain. They are just a product of the brain at work creating thoughts in the same way as the marrow creates blood. The one is no more truly under my control than the other. But then, there is really no "*I*" to control anything. If this entity I call "myself" is purely material, then there is no soul or spirit dwelling in it. My brain is deluded when it imagines that there is a person dwelling in this body who is something more than a parcel of flesh, blood, and bones. In fact, there is nothing here but a slowly decaying mass of temporarily energised matter, which has no destiny except to provide a banquet for worms.

Is it possible that anyone could ever truly hold such ideas about themselves? Well, there *are* certain atheists and others who have been brave enough to put their drab notions into print. But do they really *believe* what they write? Their actions and their life-style show otherwise. Whatever they may *say*, they continue to *behave* as if they were as much subject to an external moral law as the most devout worshipper.

We feel, then, that we are on solid ground when we assert with great confidence that the moral law truly does exist apart from and beyond us, eternal in heaven, and that it expresses itself through the persistent voice of human conscience.

But consider this. The concept of a universal and eternal moral law is an "idea"; but ideas can exist only in a *mind*. Whose mind first conceived the moral law? Our answer, of course, is God; for if not him, then who?

Someone might protest that *everything* (material and immaterial) can be described as an "idea", and in a sense that would be true. But moral law has a conceptual quality that distinguishes it from thoughts about an artifact. A rabbit surveying a burrow is not the same as a lawyer thinking about justice. It is barely possible to imagine the material world being its own cause, matter producing matter (as a materialist would say); but only thought can produce thought. Yet thought *cannot* exist without a mind. So once again we ask: what other source for the moral law can there be, except the mind of God? As Francis Bacon said -

> "I had rather believe all the fables in the legends and the Talmud and the Alcoran, than that this universal frame is without a Mind."[151]

---

[151] English philosopher and statesman, in an <u>Essay on Atheism</u>, written in 1625.

ESSENTIAL FOR HAPPINESS

People everywhere recognise that the greatest good is not merely that they should find happiness, but rather that *happiness must be associated with virtue*. Few would admire pleasure built upon vice. At once we face two problems -

VIRTUE WITHOUT HAPPINESS

If virtue is *not* rewarded by happiness, we feel that the moral order has been violated. Many passages in *Psalms* and *Proverbs* express this dilemma. Why do the wicked prosper? Why are the righteous often crushed? Why is injustice allowed to flourish? Where can we turn for redress of life's inequities? Who will requite the poor, the enslaved, the beaten? Who will recompense the multitudes who receive wages of bitterness for a lifetime of toil? The anguish of those questions drove the ancient Hebrews away from their original simple belief. Their early doctrines held that good things happen only to the good and bad things only to the wicked. Later they came to realise that the moral ambiguities of this life can be solved only by reckoning that virtue unrewarded now *will* be rewarded in the next, and that evil overlooked now will then be punished.

HAPPINESS WITHOUT VIRTUE

People soon discover that happiness, if it is not the reward of virtue, or of the faithful performance of duty, is ashes in the mouth. Thus Kant -

> "Morality is not properly the doctrine of how we may make ourselves happy, but how we make ourselves *worthy* of happiness."[152]

---

[152] *Critique of Practical Reason*

But why should that be so? There is certainly no sufficient cause in the world of material objects to create or enforce such a principle. No other creature on earth is subject to that rule. We humans alone are constrained by it. Evolutionary forces cannot account for it, nor nuclear physics, nor some chemical process. It stands around us like a wall built by Another's hand, preventing us from ever finding true happiness apart from nobility of character and action. We cannot help but recognise that this moral harness did not originate from our own choice; we are simply obliged to accept it as the horse must yield to its bridle. In all this we see the will and wisdom of the Almighty.

VIRTUE IS REQUIRED

The best of thinkers in every civilised nation have always agreed that every person should strive for the highest good, both for the individual and for the community. The grand moral imperative that overlays our world demands this, and shows also that the highest good is attainable by all. What we *ought* to do, we *can* do; unless we are to say that the moral law is utterly capricious. It is cruel tyranny to demand what no one can perform. Justice cannot stand upon injustice; truth cannot behave deceitfully. If the moral law insists upon virtue, then it must suppose that we are able to do virtuously.

Yet here is our dilemma. We know that in fact *none* of us is able to reach that greatest good. We must conclude then either that the moral law is in fact immoral, or that there is a future life, and God, in which that greatest good will finally be achieved.

The alternative is to deny that there is any absolute moral law. But what then? Men and women become merely pieces of sentient cosmic flotsam, occupying this planet for a few decades before they vanish into total extinction. If that is so, then the only possible compensation is to extract what happiness I can from this life, free of any concern for the welfare of others. Why should *their* happiness hold any importance for me, except insofar as it may affect my own? If none of us have souls, if none have any eternal value, if we are but accidents of time, if we came from nowhere and have nowhere to go, then let us then plunder whatever happiness we can, without concern for tomorrow!

> A little season of love and laughter,
> Of light and life, and pleasure and pain,
> And a horror of outer darkness after,
> And dust returneth to dust again.[153]

But, can the man who deems himself no different in quality from a handful of dust, can the woman who sees herself perishing like a blade of grass, ever experience meaningful joy? Unremitting despair would seem a more rational response. We feel such nobility within ourselves, yet we are told that we are no more than some hideous experiment in a galactic laboratory. Poet and philosopher combine to say that when your day in the sun is done you will be cast onto the trash heap of earth's detritus. Do you believe that? Then let hopelessness possess your soul, and lament fill your days with sorrow. So said the materialist Bertrand Russell -

> "That Man is the product of causes which had no prevision of the end they were achieving; that his origin, his growth, his hopes and fears, are but the outcome of accidental collocations of atoms; that no fire, no heroism, no intensity of thought and feeling, can preserve an individual life beyond the grave; that all the labours of the ages, all the devotion, all the inspiration, all the noonday brightness of human genius, are destined to extinction in the vast death of

---

[153] From <u>The Swimmer</u>, by Adam Lindsay Gordon (1833-70), Australian poet. He died by his own hand in Melbourne.

the solar system, and that the whole temple of Man's achievement must inevitably be buried beneath the debris of a universe in ruins - all these things, if not quite beyond dispute, are yet so nearly certain, that no philosophy which rejects them can hope to stand. Only within the scaffolding of these truths, only on the firm foundation of unyielding despair, can the soul's habitation henceforth be safely built."[154]

Now that is a wondrously eloquent passage, yet it is surely absurd. How can a "religion" (for that is what it is) of "unyielding despair" ever provide a "firm foundation" upon which to build any kind of life? What is this "soul's habitation" Russell speaks about? By his philosophy we *have* no soul, we are just animals, different from other creatures only in that we are (or think we are) more intelligent. Yet that intelligence must be an awful curse if its major use is to make us unique among animals in the knowledge of our own extinction. Better to have been born an absolute imbecile, living only for each moment, with no memory of the past nor any anticipation of the future. My cat must be happier than I, as he dozes in the sun, blissfully unaware that he must die and vanish forever.

Materialists think that despite such a ruinous belief they can still build a case for a noble life. They insist that we should still aspire to virtue, searching always for a higher ethic. But we are entitled to ask: why bother? What can their philosophy teach me, except to cling to life as long as I can, avoid as much pain as possible, and live only for myself? Why should I care anything for those other bits of wandering garbage who inhabit this planet? Let me rather catch what

---

[154] The passage comes from an essay Russell wrote in 1918, but affirmed again in his "Autobiography" in 1969. Taken from Hick, op. cit. pg. 61, 62.

happiness I can, whether or not it hurts other temporary occupants of this global rubbish tip.

Will such nonsense prevail? Of course not. Materialists will be disappointed in their claim that "no philosophy which rejects (materialism) can hope to stand." Long after each clever thinker's name has been altogether forgotten the good news of salvation in Christ will still be sweeping millions of people joyously into the eternal kingdom of God!

> Mock on, mock on, Voltaire, Rousseau;[155]
> Mock on, mock on; 'tis all in vain!
> You throw the sand against the wind,
> And the wind blows it back again.
>
> And every sand becomes a gem
> Reflected in the beams divine;
> Blown back they blind the mocking eye,
> But still in Israel's paths they shine.[156]

PROGRESS IS DEMANDED

Suppose we agree that an external moral law must exist. What then? A corollary appears, that one of its aims is social improvement and progress. It seeks to bring the greatest level of justice and happiness to the greatest number of people. Yet we cannot imagine an earthly state in which progress will no longer be needed because perfection has been reached. Is the moral law then making a capricious and unrealisable demand? Must we live forever with injustice and inequity? Or does the fulfilment of the law's demand for moral perfection lie in another (and future) realm? Shall we join with those who scorn the idea of a coming Judgment? Or shall we look forward to that great Day of Punishment and Reward?

---

[155] Two famous 18th century rationalists and sceptics.
[156] William Blake (1757-1827), English poet, painter, engraver, mystic.

> Do not say, "I am hidden from God;
> No one in heaven takes any notice of me.
> Among so many people I will remain un-noticed;
> How can I matter in this great world?
>
> "Why should God care about what I do?
> Why should my actions attract his attention?
> If I sin, who is there to see me?
>
> "If I am secretly disloyal, who will know?
> Who will tell God even if I do good?
> Is not his judgment far, far away?"
>
> Those are the thoughts of someone
> with no understanding;
>
> Who else but a senseless person
> would speak such folly?[157]

The wisdom of the old rabbi reaches across nearly twenty-two centuries. We dare not ignore the demand of the moral law for a day of requitement. We agree with scripture, which declares that the present imperfect heaven and earth are but a preparatory stage. We joyfully await the arrival of the perfect new heaven and new earth, in which only righteousness will dwell.

JUSTICE MUST TRIUMPH

The disparate outworking in this life of reward and punishment demands a later accountability to some final Arbiter, which Christians say will occur on the great Day of Judgment predicted in scripture.

This requirement for justice to be done is admittedly an argument based more upon experience than reason; yet it accords with our innate sense of the fitness of things. We cannot formally demonstrate the need for injustice to be

---

[157] Sir 16:17, 21-23.

repaired, but we *feel* it should be so, in order to make sense of the moral urge, of the yearning for deserved happiness, which speaks so insistently within us. Thus James Finley writes:

> "Have you ever felt that the really evil people in the world will someday be called to task? It seems so unfair that the cheaters and liars and killers prosper in this life, while other really good people suffer and are taken advantage of. We have a fundamental intuition that things will be reversed someday. We sense in the core of our beings a God who is good and who will right all wrongs - if not in this life, then in the next."[158]

If there is any value in the above arguments - and most people find them strong enough - then we must come to this conclusion: the theist position provides the best explanation for the mysteries of human life, and especially of our inborn moral nature.

---

[158] Your Faith And You; Ave Maria Press, Notre Dame, Indiana, 1970; pg. 15.

Chapter Nine

COMMUNITY AND COSMOS

"Freedom and not servitude is the cure of anarchy; as religion, and not atheism, is the remedy for superstition."[159]

"A little philosophy inclineth man's mind to atheism, but depth in philosophy bringeth men's minds about to religion."[160]

"What is truth?" demanded Pontius Pilate. We may reply that at least it is two things: *personal*; and *religious.*

Truth is *personal*, for the idea of truth has no meaning anywhere on earth except among humans. No animal, bird, or insect, no tree, rock, or plant, has any sense either of truth or falsehood. "Truth" is not an attribute of material elements; it belongs neither to atoms nor galaxies. Truth is a human response to an inner sense of right and wrong; no "truth" exists outside of human perception - unless of course you locate it in God. But at once that changes the nature of truth, for if it results from the will of God then it becomes generic, applicable throughout the universe. Otherwise "truth" is nothing more than what each person says it is -

"I don't know what you meant by 'glory'," Alice said.

---

[159] Edmund Burke (1729-1797), British statesman and philosopher, from a speech, March 22, 1775.

[160] Francis Bacon, English philosopher and statesman, in an <u>Essay on Atheism</u>, written in 1625.

Humpty Dumpty smiled contemptuously. "Of course you don't - till I tell you. I meant 'there's a nice knock-down argument for you!'"

"But 'glory' doesn't mean 'a nice knock-down argument'," Alice objected.

"When *I* use a word," Humpty Dumpty said, in rather a scornful tone, "it means just what I choose it to mean - neither more nor less."

"The question is," said Alice, "whether you *can* make words mean so many different things."

"The question is," said Humpty Dumpty, "which is to be the master - that's all."[161]

The question has not changed. Who will be the master? Subjective opinion? Or an objective body of "truth" that cannot be changed by any human work? Does truth reside in me, or in God? In fact, we cannot help but feel that truth is universal, demanding obedience from the entire creation. Yet it remains *personal*, for it cannot arise out of merely physical elements. Truth can be appreciated only by a person, and must therefore have a personal source. But if ultimate truth is both personal and universal, where else can we locate it except in the mind of God?[162]

---

[161] Lewis Carroll, <u>Through the Looking-Glass</u>, Chapter Six, "Humpty Dumpty".

[162] Even at the divine level truth would be a meaningless concept unless there were another to share it. Thus truth coheres within the Godhead by means of its communication to each other by the Father, Son, and Holy Spirit. Were God uni-personal truth could not have existed. The Almighty could simply have decreed whatever and whenever he wanted to decree. But as soon as another person is involved, a standard must be set. Thus Thoreau wrote: "It takes two to speak the truth - one to speak, and another to hear." <u>A Week on the Concord and Merrimack Rivers</u> - "Wednesday"; Heritage Press, Norwalk CT, 1975; originally published in 1849.

Notice also: if it is true that without God, all truth becomes particular, then anyone who universalises truth is acknowledging (knowingly or unknowingly) the fiat of God. Jesus highlighted this remarkable personal quality when he located "truth", not in a set of propositions, but in *himself* - *"I am the truth!"* There is no final discovery of truth without the discovery of God. Reject God, and you reject all possibility of discovering what is truth.

Second, truth is also *religious*; that is, it springs out of the irresistible urge every person has toward a system of belief. No individual of ordinary intelligence can endure to live without believing in *something*. Willingly or not, we all find that we *must* make certain decisions about who we are, where we came from, and where we are going. Many people make those choices unconsciously, simply following the pressures of the surrounding culture, but make them they do. This powerful religious factor in the makeup of every man and woman has led thinkers to develop

THE SOCIOLOGICAL ARGUMENT

> "Religion is not a popular error; it is a great instinctive truth, sensed by the people, expressed by the people."[163]

The sociological argument is based upon the universal existence of religious belief and practice. As far as scholars can learn, there has never been any society without some kind of religious belief. Religious experience is common to the entire human race. And what is true collectively is also true individually: *every* person is religious, even if his or her creed is no more than belief in their own materialism (which is a dogma no more amenable than any other to strict rational proof). So atheists, since they adhere to a system of

---

[163] Ernest Renan, French historian, Les Apotres, written in 1866.

belief, may also be called "religious" - even if they do lack any god except self. However, let us allow for the moment that atheists are *not* religious, which separates them radically from the remainder of the human race, who are insatiably religious. At once we find ourselves facing

THE GREAT DIVIDE

C. S. Lewis writes -

> "I have been asked to tell you what Christians believe, and I am going to begin by telling you one thing that Christians do *not* need to believe. If you are a Christian you do not have to believe that all other religions are simply wrong all through. If you are an atheist you do have to believe that the main point in all the religions of the world is simply one huge mistake. If you are a Christian, you are free to think that all these religions, even the queerest ones, contain at least some hint of the truth. When I was an atheist I had to try to persuade myself that most of the human race have always been wrong about the question that mattered to them the most; when I became a Christian I was able to take a more liberal view. But, of course, being a Christian does mean thinking that where Christianity differs from other religions, Christianity is right and they are wrong. As in arithmetic - there is only one right answer to a sum, and all others are wrong; but some of the wrong answers are much nearer being right than others.
>
> "The first big division of humanity is into the majority who believe in some kind of God or gods, and the minority who do not. On this point, Christianity lines up with the majority - lines up with ancient Greeks and Romans, modern savages, Stoics,

Platonists, Hindus, Mohammedans, etc., against the modern western European materialist."[164]

There have been and are atheists, but there has never been a genuinely atheistic society. It seems that

"man cannot do without God, because religion is too deeply rooted in his nature, and God's revelation is too abundantly (manifest) ... Man would rather cling to the grossest kind of superstition than persist in cold and naked unbelief." [165]

Faced with such an overwhelming witness of the validity of religious belief, it requires remarkable temerity to say that the instinct of millions is wrong, and that there is no god of any sort. It is more probable that the atheist is wrong. That is why there are

FEW REAL ATHEISTS

We might even ask: "Is there any such thing as an atheist?"

There are many people who reject the *Christian* idea of God, yet they are not really atheists. In practice they deny only certain concepts of God, for they are still compelled to acknowledge some form of Absolute Power, some kind of First Cause. True theoretical, resolute, atheism, which denies the existence of absolutely anything except the material world, seldom occurs. Most people find it impossible to resist the urge to search for the cause of every phenomenon. That urge is innate to human nature. It is just one of a package of natal ideas we bring into this world, such as

> there is a difference between good and evil;

---

[164] Mere Christianity; Fontana Books; 1956; pg 39-40.
[165] Norman Geisler.

- every effect must have a cause (though it may be only a demon);
- nature can be controlled (even if only by magic);
- our minds are independent of our physical parts;
- and the like.

Those are concepts that every normal child, as he or she grows older, is irresistibly drawn to accept -

> "The moment (a child) hears these things, he cannot do differently. He voluntarily accepts these truths without asking any proof, for they are self-evident."[166]

But does not the same quality of innateness belong to the universal human religious instinct? Belief in a deity seems to be truly intuitive. Without coercion or indoctrination, prior to any kind of formal proof, most people throughout history have been drawn compulsively toward some god. Nothing is more natural than to turn one's eyes heavenward for solace, guidance, help. Prayer is instinctive in the human heart. Hence Pascal declared -

> "It is the heart, not reason, which experiences God. This then is faith: God perceived by the heart and not by reason"[167]

People do not feel that they are doing violence to their own basic nature when they go to worship; religious practice comes as easily as eating or drinking; it happens like any other normal and proper part of life. Thus Tertullian -

---

[166] Norman Geisler.

[167] Op. cit., #225.

"Diogenes, when asked ... whether there were any gods, replied: 'I do not know; only there ought to be gods'."[168]

We all feel that way. If there is no God, there *should* be! People cannot help but look for him -

> The Lord created human beings out of the dust ...
>
> He gave them a tongue, eyes, ears;
> He gave them a mind to use for thinking;
> He filled them with knowledge and wisdom;
> He taught them how to recognise both good and evil.
>
> Then he put the fear of him into their hearts
> By showing them the splendour of his works.
> He created them to be glad in him for ever,
> And to praise his holy name
> As they declard all his glorious deeds.
>
> He planted knowledge within them,
> And endowed them with the law of life,
> Revealing to them his eternal decrees,
> And establishing with them his everlasting covenant.[169]

The rabbi understood that an instinct to recognise God is built deeply into human nature. Men and women, of course, may reject the knowledge of the true God, and may worship a multitude of gods of their own making. But there are few who can altogether stifle their religious urge.

ATHEISM IS HARD WORK

What about those who do seem to lack any hunger for God? A few truly irreligious people no more disprove religion's

---

[168] Ad Nationes, Bk 2. ch 2. North African Christian apologist and lawyer (circa 200).

[169] Sir 17:1, 6-12.

reality than blindness disproves sight. Does the existence of insane people call into question the mental health of the sane?

But what about the objection that the majority of people can be, and often have been, wrong? It is true that in matters of religious dogma, vast numbers of people have at times held absurd ideas. But that is not what we are talking about. Behind the changing fashions of creeds, underlying not only the myths and legends but also the facts of religion, there remains one common all-pervading instinct: the yearning for God. Can something so universal, so endemic, so deeply embedded into human experience, be casually dismissed as a primitive irrelevance? It seems more reasonable to stand with the majority in belief. Atheists have far more need than theists to prove their case.

We may observe also that it takes conscious, even painful effort to reject deliberately all innate belief in God.[170] The mental hardship of doing so is like that of trying to cast off the ingrained idea that one is a moral being, or possesses a power of voluntary choice.[171] The reason is obvious. Those ideas all stand or fall together. If there is no God, then morality is void of meaning, and we have no more power to choose than a lump of clay (which, without God, is all that we can claim to be). That, of course, is just what the true

---

[170] There are, of course, large numbers of careless people who ignore the claims of God upon their lives, and who behave as if he were absent. Nonetheless, when pressed on the question, they will acknowledge the existence of God. Though any thought of God is usually pushed to the periphery of their daily lives, in great moments they turn to religion, such as birth, marriage, illness, death. There are very few people who can bring themselves deliberately to deny that there is a God, and to commit themselves thoroughly to a materialist view of life.

[171] As Pascal said, "Atheism shows strength of mind - but only to a certain extent." Op. cit. # 333.

materialist does assert: we are not free moral agents, but simply an assemblage of chemicals, mysteriously energised for a few years, but nonetheless fully subject to natural law.

No doubt an unbeliever, acting with cool intellectualism, can make such statements; but they cannot be made with any warmth of heart. Such a rejection of our moral nature, our freedom of choice, our spiritual yearning, ravages our deepest experience and inner awareness. That is why atheism has never been adopted by more than a handful of philosophers, along with a few others for whom the idea of God has become too troublesome.

Notice also this oddity. Atheists are quite unable to prove that God does *not* exist; yet they demand of us unassailable proof of *our* belief that he *does* exist! That demand is neither consistent nor logical. Indeed their fierce, though unfounded, rejection of God is matched in peculiarity only by their refusal to live by the utter materialism of their creed. They denounce Christianity, yet (in moral terms) continue to *live* like Christians!

BREAD OF LIFE

This endemic human desire for God suggests his existence -

> "When a person is physically hungry we know that the hunger argues for something that can satisfy it; and when man hungers after God *that* hunger argues for Someone or Something that can satisfy it. The cry, `My soul thirsteth for God` (Ps 42:2) is an argument for God's existence, for the soul would not deceive man by thirsting for something that did not exist."[172]

---

[172] Myer Pearlman, Knowing the Doctrines of the Bible, Gospel Publishing House, 1937; pg.43.

Just as the thirst for water is proof enough of its existence, so, to a spiritually sensitive person, the thirst for God compels one to his discovery. Robert Browning expressed a similar idea. The same bishop we encountered earlier is still debating with his materialist friend -

> (These) certain instincts, blind, unreasoned-out,
> You dare not set aside, you can't tell why,
> But there they are, and so you let them rule.
> Thus, friend, you seem as much a slave as I,
>
> A liar, conscious coward and hypocrite,
> Without the good the slave expects to get,
> In case he has a master after all!
> You own your instincts? Why, what else do I,
> Who want, am made for, and must have a God
>
> Ere I can be aught, do aught? No mere name
> Want, but the true thing with what proves its truth,
> To wit, a relation from that thing to me,
> Touching from head to foot - which touch I feel ... "[173]

We find ourselves, then, drawn to a conclusion that seems inescapable: either this universal belief in God, this spiritual thirst, arises from a true inherent impulse, or it results from some kind of pathological delusion in the human mind. But if that is the case, then all activity of the mind, all innate perception, becomes suspect. Why should one give credence to any opinion formed in such a diseased mind? Why should its conclusions on *any* subject be believed? But that is impossible. We cannot rationally call our own minds insane. It is more sensible to accept the evidence and to believe in God.

---

[173] Bishop Blougram's Apology

THE COSMOLOGICAL ARGUMENT

"An undevout astronomer is mad."[174]

"The universe is the language of God."[175]

The name "cosmological" comes from the Greek word for *world* ("cosmos").

If you think about it, you will realise that the previous proofs of God can all be reduced to one proposition: <u>something exists; therefore <u>God</u> exists</u>. That is the cosmological argument, and it is reckoned by many to be the major, if not the only, formal proof of God's existence. Before we search out some of its depths, here is a simple and pungent expression of the argument by Martin Luther -

> "I cannot imagine what must be going on in the mind of a man who, even though he sees the sun rise, does not firmly hold that there is a God. The question must at some time enter his mind as to whether the sun always existed, or he must be fastening his mind on the mud, like a hog. To see all those bodies move about and not to think Someone moves them is unbelievable. In other areas men know that the house does not build itself."[176]

The position, then, is really this: if the *cosmological argument* is found inadequate, then the existence of God *cannot* be formally or philosophically demonstrated. But neither can anyone prove by logic (that is, pure thought) alone that God does *not* exist. Furthermore, as we have seen, it is just as impossible to *prove* that the perceived world exists; but do we really *need* that kind of proof? Any sensible

---

[174] Edward Young (1683-1765).
[175] Lorenz Oken (1779-1851).
[176] <u>What Luther Says</u>, Vol 2, pg 538.

person will reckon that no more evidence is necessary than what we all see and touch every day. Could you seriously question the existence of the earth without being called a lunatic?

Therefore the *cosmological argument* (along with all the other "proofs") does not depend upon pure argument, but rather upon a mixture of experience with argument - with *experience* actually having the prior place. Mark that in the end even the purest thought must begin with *experience*; it can never begin with thought alone, for without an experience of some sort there is nothing to think about. That was the great proposition upon which Descartes built his philosophy and his argument for the existence of God -

> "The possibility of certain knowledge depends upon getting beyond the point of skepticism; and this can be done only, if at all, through pushing skepticism to its final limits. One is sometimes deceived by his senses. How does one know that is not a constant occurrence? How does one know that an evil genius is not deceiving him at every moment, and in every way, with respect both to external and internal appearances? If this is so, only one thing is certain: namely, that nothing is certain. "But if one is doubtful of everything, he must exist to do that doubting. Hence we come to the famous formula, `Cogito, ergo sum!'* To say, *`I think, therefore I am!'* is to assert that there is at least one proposition that can stand against the skepticism of doubt."[177]

---

[177] Illustration: take a blind baby and keep it isolated from every possible sensory perception. Even if it grew up in possession of the world's most brilliant mind, how much could it hope to discover by thought alone? The Bible position is that this is just how we stand with God: sin has blinded and deadened our ability to perceive God.
Continued on next page

Starting with himself as a thinking person, Descartes traced a path to belief in God. In effect, he formed the syllogism: *"If I exist, God exists. I do exist, therefore God exists."* Note that Descartes acknowledges that while it may be *logically* possible to deny the existence of everything (or at least to deny the reliability of our perceptions), it is *experientially* impossible for us to do so. Thus we may form another syllogism: *"If the world exists, God exists. I experience the world, and cannot deny its existence. Therefore, God exists."* Neither of those syllogisms is infallible. Shadows of logical doubt lie over the premises upon which their conclusions are built. But they remain quite strong enough to establish the reasonableness of belief in God.

CHANGING AND CONTINGENT

Not only do I exist; I also *change*: therefore I am a *finite* being, and a *contingent* being. A contingent being is one which *can*, but *need not*, exist; there is no intelligent explanation for its existence within the being itself. It has been called into existence by another. That means I came into existence by some cause outside of myself, and can also go out of it; and at every point I find myself susceptible to change and totally dependent upon some kind of external sustaining power. My contingency is complete.

Furthermore, I not only lack the power to cause my own existence, I cannot even be sure of being able to end that existence. I may destroy my body. But does that destroy *me*? I have no way of knowing. So here I am, helpless both to originate or terminate my own existence.

Continued

Unless he chooses to reveal himself to us, thought alone will never bring us to heaven.

What does that mean? It inevitably leads on to the statement: the presence of every limited, dependent, changing being, points to another cause.

The principle is technically that of "having a sufficient cause for every actualised potential". Or, a little differently: "the actualisation of any potential is intelligible only on the basis of an independent and adequate cause". For example: a moving car is an actualised potential; but so is the car itself; and then its builders; and then its designers, and so on, back further, and further, still looking for the First Cause.

That leads to another corollary: it is more *logical* for a contingent being or object *not* to exist than for it to come into existence. Think of any artifact you like - a house, car, book, or anything else. Which is more probable: that it should, or should not, exist? Given the vastness of the universe, and the expanse of time, the odds *against* your artifact coming into existence just now are immeasurable. There would be no rational way to account for it, except to say that it is here by design. Or here is another, more subtle, example. A piece of iron has a potential to be hot; but it may be expected to remain cold unless heat is artificially produced in it. However, there is no obvious reason why iron could not exist in an already heated state. So both the existence of the *potential* iron possesses to be either hot or cold, and the *actualisation* of that potential in a normally cold condition, are intelligible only on the basis of an independent cause. What, or who, is that cause? Theists say that *the only adequate cause of the actualised potential represented by iron, and thence by the entire universe, is God.*

Some try to overcome that argument by positing an *Infinite Series* of causes. But think about a long line of moving railway trucks: it is ridiculous to explain their movement by saying only that the first truck pulls the second, which pulls the third, and so on, without end. We are compelled to say finally that a locomotive pulls the entire train. Even if it were possible to think of the *line* of trucks stretching to infinity, that would still leave their *motion* unexplained, and we could not help but look for an independent source of that motion. So with the constantly moving and changing processes that are occurring around us: those processes are intelligible only if we can assign them an *"independent source of motion, outside of the system itself."*

But still someone might object: "Does our belief that the train must have a locomotive rest upon logic, or rather upon experience? And is it really impossible for there to be an infinite series of causes?" Now that criticism has value in reducing the issues to two alternatives. It forces us to say either that

- ➢ the universe *is* simply inexplicable, irrational, contrary to all our experience and sense of the fitness of things; or,
- ➢ the universe *can* be explained in terms of an *Unmoved Mover*, of one original, uncaused *First Cause*, who to us, of course, is God.

Or, if you prefer more philosophical language -

> "If the existence of the universe is an ultimately intelligible fact, it must be so by reference to a reality whose existence and character is self-explanatory, and whose relation to the space-time universe provides a sufficient reason for the latter's existence."[178]

Some would say that the above arguments just push the problem back to God himself: after all, where does *he* come from? Surely an *Uncaused Cause* is finally just as

---

[178] Hick, op. cit., pg 45; see also 47-52.

inconceivable as an *Infinite Series* of causes? That is true, except for two things:

(1) Daily observation disposes us to accept the former more readily than the latter; that is, we are more able to accept the existence of *mind* than of *things* without explanation.

> "The only way the move can be made from non-existence to existence is by an existing cause of existence. And since that *Cause* cannot be the cause of its own existence, then it must always have existed."[179]

(2) Any person who has an innate sense of the reality and presence of God, a God-awareness, will never be persuaded to exchange that personal consciousness for an impersonal physical universe. Either God is our Father, or the earth is our Mother. But God is personal, the universe impersonal; God is spiritual, the earth is material; God possesses mind, the earth is mindless. I will always choose the personal Divine Father in preference to an impersonal Earth Mother. Are we not all profoundly convinced that we are more than just a collection of molecules and chemical processes? How then could we have sprung from soulless dirt alone? No atheist has any solution for that dilemma. Hence Renford Barmbrough, commenting on *"the philosopher's besetting sin of unreality,"* cites a saying from Bertrand Russell: "I cannot see how to refute the arguments for the subjectivity of ethical values, but I find myself incapable of believing that all that is wrong with wanton cruelty is that I don't like it."[180]

---

[179] Norman Geisling, op. cit.
[180] I have lost the source of this passage.

Yet what else *can* a materialist say? Moral behaviour is impossible for amoral earth, which is all we are if we are not made by God. If I am so blind that I cannot see the handiwork of God in a fluffy kitten, or discern his majesty in the roar of thunder, or glimpse his beauty in a radiant sunset, then at least let me look at myself. Try to plumb the depths of the human spirit. Observe the glory and tragedy of human history, the nobility and wretchedness of human behaviour. Search where I will, I can find no better explanation of these mysteries than the one given in scripture: I am made in the image of God; I have been corrupted by sin; Christ died to redeem me; now I am destined for eternal glory.

VOCAL AND INTELLIGENT

One of the most baffling mysteries of human life is our power of speech. Is this merely a learned skill, or is it innate? Is it just a mechanistic process, or does it reflect something deeply fundamental to what it means to be human?

For many years linguists believed that infants learned how to talk solely by trial and error. That comfortable notion has now been dispelled. Few linguists today doubt that a capacity for language is a universal instinct, yet unique to the human species. It is now widely accepted that all human languages are governed by a genetically determined universal grammar, which is present at birth in every normal child. Where does it come from? Outside the biblical explanation (that our power of speech is a gift from God) the question does not and cannot have any adequate answer.

That is such a startling notion, it deserves serious reflection.

The evidence strongly suggests that language is not just a collection of imitated sounds, but rather depends upon "an innate knowledge of linguistic structure that is part of the genetic birthright of any normal child."[181] Language, therefore, is not just a product of environment (except that *which* language a person speaks is obviously culturally determined), but is rather inherent in the very fibre of our being.

This can be illustrated by asking how children learn to talk. The obvious reply, that they copy their parents and siblings, falls under the objection of "a poverty of stimulus" (as Casti calls it). That is, "the child is not exposed to enough language to account for the linguistic ability displayed by any normal six-year old. "In short, children's ability to use their native language is vastly under-determined by the data."[182] What are those data? Snatches of conversation, "baby talk", ill-formed words and sentences, half-stated ideas, all mixed up with careful speech, complete statements, questions, nonsense words, teasing, and the like. Yet out of it all, a child swiftly emerges with an ability to construct sentences he or she has never heard before. Further, the child instinctively masters grammar, and is able, without being aware of it, to apply rules of grammar it is not consciously aware of to new sentences, along with a sensitivity to humour, sarcasm, ambiguity, and other speech factors. And all this in contexts in which the child has never before heard such expressions.

Little of that remarkable ability can be attributed to imitation. Instead it seems undeniably to arise from catalysts that are built into each child's very genes. So the question must be asked: what is the source of these congenital skills that enable a child to surpass so greatly the poor level of instruction it receives? How can it build this

---

[181] John L. Casti, "Paradigms Lost"; Cardinal Books, London 1989; pg. 212.

[182] Ibid. pg. 216.

complex and infinite capacity for expression upon such an inadequate external foundation?

Charles Dodgson[183] captured this mystery in his "Jabberwocky" poem, which Alice is reading -

> 'Twas brillig, and the slithy toves
> Did gyre and gimble in the wabe:
> All mimsy were the borogroves,
> And the mome raths outgrabe. ...
>
> And, as in uffish thought he stood,
> The Jabberwock, with eyes of flame,
> Came whiffling through the tulgey wood,
> And burbled as it came.
>
> One two! One, two! and through and through
> The vorpal blade went snicker-snack!
> He left it dead, and with its head
> He went galumphing back. ...[184]

"'It seems very pretty,' she said when she had finished it, 'but it's *rather* hard to understand! ... Somehow it seems to fill my head with ideas - only I don't exactly know what they are!'"[185]

Alice put her finger right on the problem. The lines of the poem display impeccable syntax, but they don't make any

---

[183] That is, Lewis Carroll (1832-98), who is quoted also in Chapter Seven above. The Rev Mr. Dodgson was for most of his adult life a professor of mathematics and a logician, and he wrote several books on those themes. There is a story that Queen Victoria was so delighted by "Alice in Wonderland" that she requested a copy of any other works by the author. She was rather dismayed when she received in due course Dodgson's "Syllabus of Plane Algebraical Geometry"!

[184] Stanzas One, Four, and Five.

[185] Through the Looking-Glass, Chapter One.

sense. Reading it, one experiences a strange double sensation: there is an *outward* recognition that the words are nonsense; but also an *inner* sense that it *should* mean something. That is, some deep-seated capacity to recognise true syntax searches for meaning in the poem, even though the mind at once says that its words cannot be found in any dictionary.

These things seem to show that language is not merely a learned skill, but is an integral part of our genetic blueprint. It is not just an invention of the human mind, but is inseparable from those factors that irrevocably separate men and women from all other creatures. No animal could ever be taught to speak; yet an infant does so without effort. In response to this mystery, Casti writes -

> "Of all the evidence put forward in this book for the uniqueness of humans, in my view the language acquisition case is by far the strongest. ... (That) there is a language acquisition device that is part of our genetic makeup seems far and away a more convincing explanation of the observed facts about language acquisition than any of the counter-theories (that have been offered). ... Thus my view is that the language acquisition evidence points strongly towards the position that a human being is indeed a pretty queer bird."[186]

The conclusion to that paragraph seems deflated; it fizzles out like a damp squib. I suggest that the mystery of language proves much more than that we are "queer birds". A child's inborn capacity to recognise, and even more to produce, grammatically correct and meaningful sentences, is part of the image of God in each person. It is a phenomenon for

---

[186] Op. cit. pg. 495.

which no merely physical, mechanical, or evolutionary explanation is adequate.

The first thing the Bible tells us about God, is that he speaks: *"God said, Let there be ...!"* The second thing it tells us, is that the first man and woman were made in the likeness of God - that is, in the likeness of a God who creates by the spoken word. Echoes of that original act of creation still sound whenever a person speaks today. My words, especially when they are words of faith, mark me as a child of God.

ADDENDA

ALL THINGS WISE AND WONDERFUL

Here is another view of some of the things in human life and in the world around us that defy natural explanation -

1. LIFE

The best efforts of modern science have shown that the statistical probability of all the factors that are required to sustain life on this planet occurring accidentally is infinitesimally small. So small, I would say, that they defy rational acceptance. But if life did not occur by accident, then it must have arisen by design, which leads one irresistibly to God.

2. SOCIETY

How shall we explain human social organisation, our great cities, our amazingly diverse cultures, our many languages? Is all this just a product of environment, of haphazard collisions by atoms, or random blasts of nuclear radiation? A growing body of evidence points rather toward an innate source. We are born with this pattern already deeply embedded in our genetic structure. It is not acquired by learning, nor by experience; it is a biological gift, implanted at the beginning of human history. Evolutionary theory provides no solution to its origin. It carries rather the finger print of the Almighty.

3. LANGUAGE

Remember again the discussion a couple of pages back on the mystery of language. This too appears to have a genetic, not environmental, origin. It is an inherent gift. The best efforts of sociologists, linguists, evolutionists, have been unable to show how a small child can acquire skilled use of virtually any language so quickly. Biologists have discovered a great deal about the mechanics of how a child goes about learning the language of its parents. But *why* the child is able to do this? And *how* is the child able to make those astonishing leaps from what it has heard into creative use of the language? Any parent knows what I mean. Suddenly, seemingly out of nowhere, a child will use a sentence in a different way, or put words together with such remarkable inventive clarity, or express an idea that extends beyond the child's previous experience. Children sometimes show unexpected perception. There is a story that Lewis Carroll, who delighted in logical puzzles, after putting an apple into a little girl's right hand, asked her to look into a mirror and tell him what hand was holding the apple. With a puzzled frown, the child said, "The left hand." When she was asked to solve the mystery, she replied that if she stood *behind* the mirror the apple would again be in her right hand. Carroll said he had never heard a better answer!

This language capacity seems inexplicable; unless of course it is indeed innate, that is, put there by God.

4. REASON

One uncanny discovery of modern times has been that all the various forms of reasoning we will ever need or use are present in our minds from the moment of birth. A baby arrives with its brain already programmed to think logically, to arrange ideas into their proper sequence, to think matters through. Growing up does not create this faculty in us, but merely teaches us how to use what our minds already possess. This quality of intelligence possessed by humans is unique to us; no animal has it; it does not seem to exist anywhere else in the universe; it cannot be replicated in a machine. There is no known evolutionary process that can provide a sufficient explanation of this faculty. It is simply there. Theists naturally find its source in God. There does not appear to be any other explanation.

5. QUANTUM

Quantum theory, with its bizarre and incomprehensible notions, at least inextricably involves each observer with the universe. An impression is conveyed that one cannot exist without the other, as though universe and observer are mutually dependent. It seems that the universe came into existence just for us, and is destined to be controlled by us. Which, of course, is the biblical view.

CONCLUSION

FAITH IS A CHOICE

> "The proofs of our religion are of such a nature that they cannot be described as absolutely convincing. But they are also of such a kind that one cannot say it is unreasonable to believe them. ... The evidence, however, is such that it surpasses, or at least equals, the evidence to the contrary."[187]

Our examination of the five classic "proofs" of God has spanned the whole universe: the world of contingent objects; the world of order; the world of beauty; the moral world; the world of ideas. Yet in the end, as the previous chapter showed, they all reduce to one simple statement: *something exists; therefore God exists.*

That proposition cannot be finally "proved". Our arguments are not "proofs" in the absolute sense of the word; they are not so much a *cause* of faith as a *product* of it; they have more value to a believer than to an unbeliever - they tend to gain in force in proportion to one's already existing faith. Hence Thomas Carlyle, though he was a theist, not only rejected atheism, but also the classic proofs -

> "For out of this that we call Atheism comes so many other `isms' and falsities, each falsity with its misery at its heels! - A SOUL is not like wind contained within a capsule; the ALMIGHTY MAKER is not like a Clockmaker that once, in old immemorial ages, having made his Horologe of a Universe, sits ever since and sees it go! Not at all. Hence comes

---

[187] Blaise Pascal, op. cit. # 736, 309.

> Atheism; come, as we may say, many other `isms' ... (the) sad root of all woes whatsoever. For indeed, as no man ever saw the above-said wind-element enclosed within its capsule, and finds it at bottom more deniable than conceivable; so too he finds ... your Clockmaker Almighty an entirely questionable affair, a deniable affair ..."[188]

However, to follow Carlyle (and others) in rejecting the proofs altogether seems too harsh. At least they show that theism is not *unreasonable*, that it is *rational* to believe in God, and that God has provided in the world around us a quantity of evidence of his existence.

Avoid the mistake also of thinking that God has disclosed only enough of himself to tantalise us, but that thoughtful people must despair of ever truly discovering him -

> "God may be hidden to the worldly wise and proud; but he is ever revealed to the humble who seek his grace."

Nor should you fall into the error of thinking that the evidence is so great as to coerce belief, even for a believer. God does not give such proof of himself that doubt is no longer possible; he does not compel faith:

> "Having made man as a person in his own image, (God) always treats men as persons, respecting their relative freedom and autonomy. He does not override the human mind by revealing himself in over-whelming majesty and power, but always approaches us in ways that leave room for an uncompelled response of human faith. ... " As Pascal put it -

---

[188] Selected Writings; edited by Alan Shelston; Penguin Books, 1980; pg 278-279; and for a slightly different perspective, see also pg 250-252

> "Willing to appear openly to those who seek him with all their heart, and to be hidden from those who flee from him with all their heart, (God) so regulates the knowledge of himself that he has given indications of himself which are visible to those who seek him but not to those who do not seek him. There is enough light for those who only desire to see, and enough obscurity for those who have a contrary disposition."[189]

Thus the "proofs" of God in the end are valuable mostly as adjuncts to the witness of scripture. For that reason, many people, whose faith is already simple, untroubled, and firm, find no use for these proofs. But others are not so fortunate, and for them the proofs are an encouragement to faith, and a stiller of doubts. Even if you do not need them yourself, then, you may meet someone who does, so it is worthwhile to master them.

I have said that most people, either consciously or unconsciously, do allow the force of the "proofs", and they do believe in some god. However, the "proofs" do not oblige anyone to believe in the *Christian* God, nor to offer him any special love or obedience. Here is a graphic example from the pen of the Roman philosopher Seneca (circa 5 B.C. - A.D. 65). The passage actually deals with the folly of placing too much value upon worthless things, but in it Seneca reveals the gropings of a thoughtful pagan toward God. He knows there is a Creator, but who, where, what, he cannot tell -

> "It was, I am sure, the very intention of the creator of the world, whoever he was - whether omnipotent God, or an incorporeal reason capable of an immense creative design, or a divine spirit of life

---

[189] Hick, op. cit, pg 104. The piece from the "Pensees" is # 309 (op. cit.).

breathing its purposes alike into all things great and small, or a blind necessity, an inevitable chain of linked causes and effects - it was the intention of the creator that none but a man's most worthless possessions should ever pass into the control of another man. All that is most valuable to a man lies beyond the reach of other men's power."[190]

The evidence for one wise, good, and great Deity is greater than Seneca's vagueness implies; yet that evidence cannot by itself lead to the God of scripture. Hence the real argument we have with the world (and with other religions) is not so much about *God* as it is about the *Bible*, and especially, how true is the gospel? At once we realise that the greatest proof to unbelievers must be, not clever argument, but personal testimony. That is why Jesus commanded his disciples to *"Go and tell everyone about the great things God has done for you"* (Mk 5:19; etc). It was sound counsel. In almost every field, apologists recognise that "proof" will convince people only when they are already disposed to believe. Why? Because our deepest need is emotional, not rational; our hearts must be stirred before our intellects will respond.

Has anyone ever been drawn to faith by argument alone? Probably not. Therefore, once again, the command of Christ to his church is: *"Preach the gospel,"* not *"Debate philosophy."* Debate has its proper place, and the proofs of God have their proper use. But the Christian's real confidence must rest in *proclamation* and *witness* rather than in argument. Never forget: the Holy Spirit has promised to confirm only the Word! So let Paul end the matter for us -

---

[190] <u>Seneca: Four Tragedies and Octavia</u>, tr. E. F. Watling; Penguin Books, 1966. From "Appendix II, #2, Consolations in Exile" (*Ad Helviam Matrem* VIII); pg. 314.

"When I came to you, my friends, to tell you about the mystery of God, I did not bring fine eloquence or lofty wisdom. I was determined to know nothing among you except Jesus Christ, and him crucified. ... Neither my preaching nor my message depended upon cleverly persuasive words. Instead, I brought you a demonstration of the Spirit's power, so that your faith might be built, not upon human wisdom, but upon the power of God." (1 Co 2:1-5).

BIBLIOGRAPHY

Age of Scandal, The; The Folio Society, London, 1993.

Alfred, Lord Tennyson; *In Memoriam; Tennyson's Poetry;* Ed. Robert W. Hill Jr. W.W. Norton & Co. New York, 1850.

Bettenson, Henry; Ed. *Documents of the Christian Church*; Oxford University Press, London, 1975.

Bettenson, Henry; David Knowles Tr.; *City of God;* Penguin Books, London, 1977.

Carlyle, Thomas; *Sartor Resartus*; J. M. Dent & Sons Ltd.; London, 1908.

Carroll, Lewis (1832-98); (Rev Charles Dodgson); *The Annotated Alice*; Bramhall House; New York, 1960.

Casti, John L.; *Paradigms Lost*; Cardinal Books; London, 1989.

Cervantes, Miguel; Tr. J. M. Cohen; *Don Quixote*; Penguin Books, 1956.

Descarte; Discourse on Method; 1637.

Donne, John (1572-1631), Poem; *To the Countess of Bedford*; The Complete English Poems; Ed. A. J. Smith; Penguin Books, 1971.

Emerson, Ralph Waldo; *Introduction to Nature*; James Munro & Co.; 1836.

Finley, James; *Your Faith And You*; Ave Maria Press; Notre Dame, Indiana, 1970.

Gordon, Adam Lindsay (1833-70); Poem; *The Swimmer*.

Hick, J. H.; *Arguments For The Existence Of God*; McMillan Press, London, 1979.

Hofstadter, Douglas; *Goedel, Escher, Bach;* Vintage Books, N.Y. 1979.

Jastrow, Robert; *God And The Astronomers*. W.W. Norton; New York, 1978.

Kant, Immanuel; *Critique Of Pure Reason*; 1781.

Kerenyi, C.; *The God's of the Greeks;* Thames and Hudson; 1988.

Khayyam, Omar; *Rubaiyat;* (c. 1100).

Kingsley, Charles (1819-1875); *The Water Babies*. Macmillan's Magazine (1862-63).

Lewis, C. S.; *Mere Christianity*; Fontana Books; 1956.

Lindsell, Harold; *The Battle For The Bible;* Zondervan; 1976.

Lytton, Lord; The Last of the Barons.

Morris, Ivan; Tr.; *The Pillow Book Of Sei Shonagon*; Penguin Classics, 1967.

Paley, William (1743-1805); *Natural Theology*; 1802.

Pascal, Blaise; (1623-62) *Penses;* Tr. John Warrington; J. M. Dent & Sons Ltd, London, 1973.

Patrides, C. A.; The Major Works; *Introduction to Sir Thomas Browne*; Penguin Books, 1977.

Pearlman, Myer; *Knowing the Doctrines of the Bible*; Gospel Publishing House, 1937.

Plass E. M.; Compiled; *What Luther Says*; Concordia Publishing House, 1959.

Reese; W. L.; Ed. *The Dictionary of Philosophy and Religion*; Harvester Press, Sussex; 1980.

Renan, Ernest; *Les Apotres*; French historian, 1866.

Romans and Their Gods, The; W. W. Norton and Co.; New York, 1969.

Russell, Bertrand; *Autobiography,* Routledge Classics; 1950.

_____; History of Western Philosophy; 1945.

_____; *Why I Am Not A Christian*; Unwin Books, London, 1975.

Sartor Resartus; J. M. Dent & Sons, London, 1913.

Schaff, Philip; Ed.; *Nicene and Post-Nicene Fathers*; Eerdman's Pub. Co. reprint, 1979.

Seneca; Tr. E. F. Watling; *Four Tragedies and Octavia*; Penguin Books, 1966.

Service, Robert; *Ballads of a Bohemian*; T. Fisher Unwin; London, 1921.

Shelston, Alan; Ed.; *Selected Writings*; Penguin Books; 1980.

Sirach; Apocrypha.

Staniforth, Maxwell; Tr. *Meditations*; Penguin Books, 1986.

Thoreau, Henry David; *A Week on the Concord and Merrimack Rivers*, Norwalk CT., 1975.

Turnbull, Ralph G.; *Baker's Dictionary of Practical Theology*; Baker Book House, Grand Rapids, Michigan. 1978.

Virgil; *The Georgics*; Tr. Folio Society, London, 1969.

Whitehead, Alfred North & Bertrand Russell; *The Principia Mathematic;* Cambridge University Press; 1963.

Wieland, C. M. (1733-1814); *Musarion;* 1768.

Wilde, Oscar; *Garden Of Eros;* 1881.

ANCIENT TEXTS

Augustine, The City of God
Cicero; *De Divinatione*; (B.C. 106-43).
Nicene and Post Nicene Fathers

MAGAZINE ARTICLES

Boslough John; National Geographic Magazine; Art.; *Worlds Within The Atom*; May 1985.

Bush, Vannevar; Dr.; Fortune Magazine; Art.; *Science Pauses*; May 1965.

Clark, Gordon H. Professor; Christianity Today Magazine; Art.; *Philosophy Of Science and Belief in God.*

Economist, The; Art.; March 11, 1989.

Galileo Affair, The; Scientific American; Art.; August 1982.

Goodwin, Kenneth O. Dr.; Adelaide Advertiser; Art.; c. 1980.

Jaki Stanley L. Dr.; Christian Century; Art.; *Science: From the Womb of Religion*; October 7, 1987.

Jastrow, Robert; Christianity Today Magazine; Art.; *A Scientist Caught Between Two Faiths*; Aug 6, 1982. .

Livingstone, David N.; Christian Scholar's Review; Art.; *Evolution As Metaphor and Myth*; 1983.

Shaken Atheism: A Look at the Fine-Tuned Universe; Christianity Today Magazine; Art.; Dec. 3rd, 1986.

Visions Of A New Faith; Science Digest; Art.; Nov 1981.

www.ingramcontent.com/pod-product-compliance
Lightning Source LLC
Chambersburg PA
CBHW051052160426
43193CB00010B/1156